MARKETING

THE BASICS

Karl Moore and Niketh Pareek

Routledge
Taylor & Francis Group

LONDON AND NEW YORK

First published 2006
by Routledge
2 Park Square, Milton Park, Abingdon, Oxon OX14 4RN

Simultaneously published in the USA and Canada
by Routledge
270 Madison Ave, New York, NY 10016

Routledge is an imprint of the Taylor & Francis Group, an informa business

© 2006 Karl Moore and Niketh Pareek

Typeset in Aldus Roman and Scala Sans by
Taylor & Francis Books
Printed and bound in Great Britain by
MPG Books Ltd, Bodmin, Cornwall

British Library Cataloguing in Publication Data
A catalogue record for this book is available from the British Library

Library of Congress Cataloging in Publication Data
A catalog record for this book has been applied for

ISBN10: 0-415-38080-4 (hbk)
ISBN10: 0-415-38079-0 (pbk)
ISBN10: 0-203-96751-8 (ebk)

ISBN13: 978-0-415-38080-5 (hbk)
ISBN13: 978-0-415-38079-9 (pbk)
ISBN13: 978-0-203-96751-5 (ebk)

MARKETING

THE BASICS

Th marketing manager of tomorrow must think in international terms in
ord r to keep up with increasingly unpredictable consumer behaviour.
Co petition in business today is fierce and you need to know how to
cap ure and keep hold of your target audience. This book includes all the
vit information you need to excel and covers:

- The role of the manager
- Marketing as a corporate function
- How to analyse competitors
- Market research
- Models of consumer behaviour
- Global marketing

1   book is ideal for any student or practitioner wanting to learn the
f   amentals of marketing applied in a global context.

K l Moore is a Professor in Marketing Strategy at McGill University and
a   sociate Fellow at Templeton College, Oxford University. He was recently
id   ified as being amongst a group of the "world's greatest business
thi..kers" in Business Strategy Review (Winter 2005).

Niketh Pareek is a journalist and management consultant. He specializes in
developing business models, finance and marketing research

ALSO AVAILABLE FROM ROUTLEDGE

INTERNET: THE BASICS
JASON WHITTAKER

MANAGEMENT: THE BASICS
MORGEN WITZEL

BUSINESS: THE KEY CONCEPTS
MARK VERNON

FIFTY KEY FIGURES IN MANAGEMENT
MORGEN WITZEL

THE ROUTLEDGE DICTIONARY OF BUSINESS MANAGEMENT
DAVID STATT

CONTENTS

LIST OF ILLUSTRATIONS

INTRODUCTION

Karl Moore and Niketh Pareek

In the global economy, markets are international; consequently the marketing manager of tomorrow must think in global or at least regional terms. Customers can switch suppliers at the click of a mouse; new technologies quickly render established firms obsolete; foreign competitors you never even knew existed ravage your national market share; and competition is mildly described as fierce. As globalization continues to foster closer social, economic and political ties, there is an increasing need for the new generation of marketing managers to think in an international and integrative perspective.

If only our problems were only conceptual. Wanting more free time, and convenience, customers are more sophisticated, less brand loyal and price sensitive than in the past, rendering traditional marketing approaches less effective. We find in North America and Western Europe a bifurcation of consumer's buying habits. It sounds rude, but what it means is that well off people are buying not only at their traditional upscale department stores but are also buying "cheap and cheerful" at Wal-Mart and other stores of that ilk. This is new. What is also new is that lower income people are doing the same: buying the bulk of their shopping list at inexpensive outlets but also spoiling themselves by buying at upscale stores and at spas. We are not sure they can really afford this, witness the rising burden of consumer debt in North America, but people today work longer and harder than ever, what's wrong with a little fun to break the routine? This behaviour means that consumers are harder to predict, they don't necessarily follow the more entrenched patterns of the past. New forms of marketing such as buzz and experiential marketing have gained wide accept-ance, and are for certain product launches, expected. The dominance of the old-line television networks is diminished in the 500-channel universe. TIVO and other personal recording devices subtly shift power to the consumer as they, in effect, become their own network chief. The emergence of massive online gaming worlds is transforming software companies into market research laboratories. New strategies offer new choices, but which to choose? How are these methods and indeed success measured? How does marketing strategy fit with the overall corporate strategy? The difficulties of marketing in the 21st century are real and tangible.

To encourage an international and integrative perspective, the marketing manager of tomorrow must start thinking in such dynamic terms at the onset of their education. Existing textbooks impart a sense of marketing's role in the firm. Where they too often fail is promoting a sense of internationalism and opportunism. By opportunism, we don't mean it in the self-serving sense of the word. Opportunism means recognizing and understanding how new trends are creating new opportunities. We feel they fail because textbooks are written specifically for a particular geographic region and restrict themselves to traditional "Old Economy" examples. Localizing the content traps the reader into thinking locally and acting globally, not the other way round. And telling old war stories prepares the troops for the old battles. We've been living in a new world order for over 15 years now.

Many clever marketers are beginning to use new tools like buzz and experiential marketing successfully but don't fully understand. We are still mucking about learning about them! But clearly these new basics will continue to grow in importance. We think it is important for you to be aware of these different approaches. That is why this book will take a more international and opportunistic approach to explaining the basics of marketing to our readers. We not only cover the basics but also introduce you to the "new" basics. We also try to tell a number of real life marketing stories based on our own experience as professional marketers.

ABOUT THE BOOK

At the end of every chapter we have included a brief summary, a set of critical questions, and glossary so that the reader can review the key concepts easily. Each chapter is also divided into headings which are labelled making the task of outlining much easier. In addition, we have taken great care in avoiding falling into the jargon trap that unfortunately is all too prevalent in business. Based on the feedback we've received from academics and practitioners, they've all felt the book succeeded in being comprehensively informative and easy to read. We're confident you will too.

BRIEF OUTLINE OF THE BOOK

Chapter one, "What is Marketing Management?", provides a general overview of marketing. Terms will be defined, the basics are explained and an explanation is provided for why companies become customer oriented.

Chapter two, "Marketing as a Corporate Function" introduces a basic framework of how marketing fits in an organization and the planning and analysis process managers must undertake in order to implement programs that aim to achieve the organization's goals. Special attention will be made towards explaining competitive advantage, core competencies, product and business cycles. The chapter concludes with a discussion of brands and the experiential economy. Protecting brands is causing marketers to adapt their behaviour from regimented practices to those of buzz marketing, where results are much more difficult to measure and predict.

Chapters three through six constitute the heart of the book. In these chapters readers will learn the tools marketers use to influence the revenue of a product. Specifically, we discuss the five Ps of marketing: product, placement, price, promotion, and people. We will explore each of these topics in some detail and how these variables are used to craft a successful marketing plan that will build a competitive advantage for the firm. We also discuss the new "basics" that are starting to gain widespread acceptance.

Chapter seven discusses how marketing is conducted. The reader will learn how to STP: segment, target and position. To do this, they must collect information, segment the market, and target their product to suit the needs and wants of a particular group. Consumer behaviour, demographics and lifestyle will be examined in detail, and how companies attempt to associate their brand to an experience. Buzz marketing is discussed in this chapter.

Chapter eight peers into the black box of the customer's mind. Market research is the means to STP's ends. We will compare and contrast the methodologies of various data collection techniques, such as focus groups, surveys, and simulators illustrating their benefits and drawbacks. The chapter ends with a discussion of neuromarketing, a new field that uses brain-scanning technology to measure a customer's neural response to particular imagery. It is only a matter of time before neuromarketing becomes part of the "new" basics.

We end the book with a discussion of global marketing. Chapter nine discusses the role culture plays in business and the importance for marketers to adapt the product to suit local tastes.

ABOUT THE AUTHORS

Karl worked for IBM and other high-tech giants for 11 years in sales and marketing management positions and has worked as a marketing consultant for the last 16 years. He has also taught regularly at Cambridge, Duke, The Drucker School in Claremont California, the Rotterdam School of Management, and at schools in Asia. He is an Associate Professor of Marketing Strategy at McGill University in Montreal, prior to which he was on the faculty at Oxford University from 1995–2000, where he continues as a fellow of Said Business School. The winter 2005/2006 issue of *Business Strategy Review*, published by the London Business School, identified Karl among a group of the world's greatest business thinkers. Others on the list of about 20 include: Charles Handy, Phillip Kotler, Gary Hamel, Warren Bennis and Rosabeth Moss Kanter. Niketh has worked in the Middle East and North America as a management consultant in the high-tech and entertainment industries.

WHAT IS MANAGEMENT?

Before delving into the world of marketing management, let us pause and briefly discuss what exactly management is, its history and how it has evolved through time.

Management is not only a word used to describe a group of senior executives. Management is also a philosophy. Management is the means to achieve an end. The late Peter Drucker, the doyen of management gurus, once said that, "The purpose of a business is to create a customer". If you do that well, profits will follow. For public institutions, they aim to increase social welfare for the public they serve by redistributing tax revenue. For non-governmental organizations, their goal is improving the welfare of the disadvantaged, or promoting the observance of human rights or improving the state of the natural environment. Though the goals of these three types of organization are different, which in turn means the decisions senior executives make will differ, all three operate with limited resources. As such, the approaches taken to realize their goals are remarkably similar. *Management is the coordination of activities to maximize limited resources enabling an organization to realize a stated goal or objective.*

The idea of management dates back to the beginning of civilization. The root of the word management can be traced back to Roman times. The Latin word *manum agere* literally translates as lead by the hand, but more tellingly, also means using power and jurisdiction to lead. The word management itself did not appear until the early Renaissance, with the French using the word *ménagement* to describe the art of conducting. By 1589, the word was absorbed into the English language. Less than 100 years later, the words "manager" and "management" became common words in the English vocabulary and remain so today.

During the Age of Enlightenment, an intellectual movement during the 18th Century originating in Europe, classical economists like Adam Smith and John Stuart Mill formalized ideas about satisfying human needs with limited resources. The two discussed how scarcity affected the allocation of resources, methods of production, and how goods were priced. While academics discussed problems related to scarcity, manufacturers experimented with production processes which led to an abundance of innovations:

quality-control procedures, replaceable parts and mass-production techniques quickly revealed their benefits. Mass production in particular was one of the greatest innovations of that time. It utilized assembly lines and permitted high rates of production at a very low cost. These savings in turn resulted in high quality but inexpensive products. It is because of mass production, much of the material wealth we enjoy today exists.

Mass production also fostered the creation of the multinational corporation, an organization that sought to vertically integrate itself controlling all factors of production, capturing all the profits within each production step, creating an immense amount of wealth for shareholders. However, at the same time, mass production meant workers were forced to do the same, repetitive actions day in day out, numbing both the brain and motivation. Workplace related injuries during this time were unacceptably high by today's standards.

The first comprehensive theories of management appeared in the 1920s. Henri Fayol was one of the first to explore the various branches of management and their inter-relationships. Within the next twenty years, academics from the arts and sciences began applying principles of psychology, sociology, and statistics to explain phenomena occurring in the business world. Subjects covering topics related to organizational behaviour, human resources and econometrics, began to be taught at newly opened business schools in universities such as Harvard.

Today, there are literally thousands of journals containing information on just about any issue in the field. On top of that, there are tens of thousands of trade magazines, newspapers and pamphlets that cater their reporting to a particular market. Having so much information is both a blessing and a curse. The information you seek likely exists, finding it is another story. Rest assured the marketplace of ideas does exist.

SUGGESTIONS FOR FURTHER READING

Peter Drucker, *Management: Tasks, Responsibilities, Practices*, New York, Harper & Row, 1974.

A classic by the original management guru, who recently passed away at the age of 95. His contribution to the field is immeasurable, and he will forever be remembered as being one of the most influential thinkers of his time. This is a big book and takes a while to get through. Alternatively, try the shorter essays in Drucker's *The New Realities*, New York, Harper & Row, 1989.

Henri Fayol, *General and Industrial Management*, trans. I. Gray, New York, David S. Lake, 1984.

An early attempt (the book was first published in 1917) to construct a general theory of what management is, this book has indirectly influenced much modern thinking about management.

Henry Mintzberg, *The Nature of Managerial Work*, New York, Harper & Row, 1973.

This was a revolutionary book in its day, and still runs counter to much formal management theory. The picture of how managers actually do manage, however, remains a compelling story.

WHAT IS MARKETING MANAGEMENT?

WHAT IS MARKETING MANAGEMENT?

Marketing is the intermediary between the customer and the business. The marketing department strives to profoundly understand the customer to develop a product or service which the customer will want. Once that information is gathered, that information is transferred to the business, which in turn produces a product according to those specifications. Once a product has been created, the marketing department is responsible for communicating to the consumer the benefits of the product, and points out how their product differs from the competition. For example, walk into any grocery store and pay close attention to the different brands of pasta sauces. Not only can you buy plain tomato sauce, you can buy varieties blended with peppers, mushrooms or a *mélange* of herbs. Each variant offers the consumer something the others do not. Emphasizing the differences between choices and the value the consumer will receive is the essence of marketing. Of course, the value received goes beyond the physical product. It includes the meaning of the product's brand. Many consumers will pay more for a Coke than for a generic brand of cola, even if they often cannot tell the difference in taste. Clearly the brand offers a set of benefits that extend far beyond the attributes of their product. We will take a closer look at brands later but for now we will only state that those products that add meaning and experience truly differentiate themselves in the mind of customers. In the introduction we defined management as a set of activities to help an organization realize a stated goal by maximizing limited resources. Following that definition we define marketing management as the administering of the process of satisfying consumer needs while ensuring the company makes a profit.

Marketing has two aims. The first is to attract new customers by highlighting the potential value a good or service offers a consumer. Getting customers is an active process, the business must solicit the customer. Rarely do customers come to a business.

The second aim of marketing is to retain customers by continually meeting and surpassing the customer's satisfaction with the product. Researchers have found that often as much as 80% of a company's revenue accrues from as few as 20% of a company's repeat customers. The luxury car manufacturer Lexus estimated the lifetime value of a satisfied customer was worth $1.17 million, or roughly 20 times the retail price of one car. The reasons being were that profit was accrued not from the sale of the car itself, but from the sale of spare parts and maintenance checks.

However, unless Toyota (the makers of Lexus) has managed to hide from securities regulators they are a majority shareholder in a major oil company, the cost of spare parts and maintenance checks do not add up to $1.17 million. How did Lexus come up with a figure so high? It turns out that satisfied customers are also likely to tell their friends how pleased they are with a product, a social phenomenon called **word of mouth marketing**. One of the paradoxes of urban centres is that though there's a large concentration of diverse groups, individuals living in cities tend to associate themselves only with people of a similar ilk; the person that can afford a Lexus is likely to know other people with similar incomes and tastes. And despite how much influence advertisers like to think they wield over customers, a personal endorsement plays a much larger role in a purchasing decision than any slick marketing campaign. Just take a look at Google as proof. With no formal advertising whatsoever, other than encouraging users to "spread the word", their company has grown from a tiny start-up to the market leader in Internet search engines. For Lexus, the power of a glowing recommendation is literally worth a million dollars.

THE FUNDAMENTAL PRINCIPLE OF MARKETING

The fundamental principle underlying marketing theory is that throughout the course of a day, humans instinctually seek to satisfy their intrinsic needs. Needs can be classified into three groups: physical, social or individual. Physical needs include food, shelter, and security. Social needs include a desire for companionship or acceptance within a group. Finally, self-expression and desire for knowledge are types of individual needs.

To satisfy these needs, humans must consume. Though the desire to satisfy unmet needs is instinctual, the items or actions chosen to satisfy those needs are not motivated by carnal impulses. On the contrary, the choices a person makes, called **wants**, are influenced by cultural and personal experiences. For example, if you live in East Asia, eating rice for breakfast is commonplace. In Western Europe and North America, however, a typical breakfast entails eating a grain or corn-based cereal. Wants steer purchasing decisions.

Since humans have the same needs but different wants, it opens up the possibility for many products to exist. But how does a company determine the extent of the variation? The process is called **market segmentation**.

Market segmentation entails taking a population and dividing them into groups according to a set of shared characteristics. In order to create these groups, **market research** is needed to identify the characteristics that the segment shares. Market research is the planned, systematic collection and analysis of data used by managers to make a decision. Market research provides information on a customer's preferences, their buying habits, their attitudes, likes and needs. Furthermore, market research reveals the potential size and purchasing power of the segment.

An example of segmentation is what drug firm, Pfizer, is now doing. In the past they used sales reps to call regularly on physicians to inform them about new types of therapies. However, Pfizer no longer treats all physicians alike, research revealed that many physicians did not appreciate sales reps taking up their already limited time. Physicians much prefer to evaluate information while attending seminars or during their spare time reading information published on the Internet. As such, Pfizer responded by segmenting physicians according to how they like to be communicated to. By doing so, Pfizer could better allocate their resources to the needs of each group.

Segmenting the market allows the marketer to identify which group or groups they believe are the most attractive. For any market there are many potential segments, one of the great challenges of marketing is carefully choosing a small number of segments on which to focus your limited resources. Learning to say no to opportunities is a difficult thing for many marketers to do! Even a giant like IBM has only finite resources and must carefully align them to the markets for which it has best advantages over their competitors. The segment(s) the firm decides to market their product to is called the **target market**. It is the target market that is exposed to a variety of carefully calibrated marketing strategies, what we call the five Ps (product, place, price, promotion and people). Together, the strategies chosen for the 5 Ps is known as the **marketing mix**. We will discuss market segmentation, and the marketing mix in further detail in chapters 3 through 6.

THE EIGHT STATES OF DEMAND

When individuals seek to buy a product to satisfy a need, they create *demand*. The definition of demand in marketing is the same as that used by economists. Demand is call or desire for a particular product the consumer wants to satisfy their needs. Economists assume that market demand can be aggregated, and represented on a chart using one downward sloping line. Philip Kotler, regarded as one of the most influential researchers in marketing, found that market demand is not so neatly linear. His research proved that market demand for a product actually has different states, and the state in which the market is in, in turn, determines the profitability of the product. Skilled marketers seek to influence the concentration, timing and type of demand.

1   NEGATIVE DEMAND

Negative demand arises when the targeted market dislikes the product offered. They actively avoid it, and actively dissuade others from consuming it. During the early 1990s, Nike outsourced the production of their athletic shoes to countries with extremely low workplace safety standards. Employees worked under conditions similar to sweatshops described in Charles Dickens' novels about

British industrialization. At first, Nike claimed they were not responsible for their suppliers' activities. Years of bad press and protests by social welfare groups started to affect shoe sales, causing Nike to start forcing their suppliers to allow independent inspectors audit the conditions of the sweatshops.

2   NO DEMAND

During a period of no-demand, a customer is unaware of the product or is disinterested. This type of demand is commonplace for new products that serve a need or want that the customer is unaware can be satisfied. Many call this situation a "a solution looking for a problem." To overcome this critical issue, the producer must continue to tweak the product in search of the "killer application" that satisfied the need. A good example is the 3G cellphone. Despite the widespread popularity of earlier versions of cellphones, manufacturers of the third generation, or "3G" phones as they were called, found themselves in a state of no demand; the 3G phone offered much better sound quality and reliability, however when it was released, the market hadn't fully absorbed the 2G version yet. When consumers were faced with the choice between the two, they wouldn't justify paying the extra expense. Sales of 3G took off once manufacturers started adding such features as downloadable ringtones, a digital camera and other items to personalise the phone. These features helped to create tangible differences between the 2G and 3G phone. Products are technology-driven. Markets are time-driven. Markets need time to understand what possibilities exist with new technology.

3   LATENT DEMAND

A market is in a period of latent demand when existing products fail to completely satisfy customer need. This occurs due to a variety of reasons: it is not economically feasible, the technology hasn't been invented yet, the producer misunderstands their customer, or the customer cannot express their need clearly. Producers actively scan the economy for markets with latent demand. They are extremely attractive because there are willing buyers. The automobile industry is a perfect example of a market with latent demand. For over two generations, environmentally-concerned consumers have experienced what psychologies call a **cognitive dissonance**. These drivers need to drive a vehicle daily, yet experience a sense of guilt or remorse since they know they contribute to global warming. To overcome this sense of conflict, they want automobile manufacturers to sell a zero-emission vehicle. Such a vehicle could have been built 30 years ago using batteries and electric motors, however, it never would have satisfied the safety and performance needs of environmentally-conscious drivers. Batteries do not produce as much power as quickly or as cheaply as gasoline. Imagine if such a car was built. Automobile manufacturers could raise prices as high as the lifetime cost of fueling the vehicle.

4   DECLINING DEMAND

Declining demand occurs when customers are losing interest in the good or service because of changing attitudes, tastes, or cultural trends. Although there are many warning signs a market is experiencing declining demand, even the world's best marketers can miss the early indicators. In 2003, McDonald's announced their first loss in their corporate history. Management didn't understand that consumers were extremely concerned about reducing their caloric intake. Obesity levels in the Western world have skyrocketed over the last two decades. As a consequence, McDonald's loyal customers increasingly chose to eat lower caloric but healthier foods such as salads, and low-carbohydrate foods, items that were not as profitable as their fried food options. What's more, many customers stopped visiting altogether because they were fed up with persistent requests to supersize their portion. Supersizing is a profitable practice for a restaurant. It is a selling strategy that entails suggesting to a client to choose a larger portion size for a proportionately smaller increase in cost. The restaurant benefits because they fatten their margin, and the customer benefits because they feel they're getting more value for their money. Morgan Spurlock's 2004 movie *Supersize Me* detailed this practice quite poignantly.

During times of declining demand, marketers must uncover the roots of the malaise and refocus the marketing mix. McDonald's is trying to do that by offering salads, working to remove trans-fats from their foods, and offering new products for adults that include salad, bottled water and a pedometer. Their famous Happy Meal, which is targeted to children, now includes a fruit and milk option. Finally, they publish nutrition and suggested lifestyle changes for people concerned about their health.

5   IRREGULAR DEMAND

Many organizations face irregular demand because their sales are correlated to a particular season, the time of day, or the whims of shoppers. For example department stores continually lose money until the Christmas season, which is where the bulk of the profits are made and the other 11 months of operation is paid for. To smooth out the variation, a marketer must find ways to encourage consumers to buy during low-peak times. Many movie theatres now offer cheaper tickets on Tuesday nights to encourage people to fill seats on what was the slower night of the week for many years. The Hawaiian tourism board knows that April is the quietest time for visitors to come to their islands. They recently started a new campaign in 2005, Hawaii Arts, to draw visitors during April. Focusing on the rich existing arts scene in Honolulu and surrounding area they advertise in the *Smithsonian Magazine* and the *New Yorker*, upscale magazines popular with the East Coast upper income class. This campaign has been quite been successful drawing additional visitors during their slowest month.

6   FULL DEMAND

Full demand situations arise when the company is selling as much as they expected the market could bear. In this type of market, marketers need only maintain the current level of demand by modifying the marketing mix accordingly..

7   OVERFULL DEMAND

Overfull demand arises when the market demand exceeds supply. Such a situation is initially good for sellers. Not only is the company selling their entire inventory, the shortage is pushing prices higher, and potentially creates a frenzied atmosphere around the product. When Haagen Daaz first started selling a green-tea ice cream in Japan, it became a must-have product. People lined up for hours outside of ice cream parlours, waiting patiently to eat this much-sought dessert. Overfull demand is an envious situation, and if left unprotected, competition will enter the market.

8 UNWHOLESOME DEMAND

Products that are harmful to society, but are still demanded by consumers create a market characterized by unwholesome demand. Marketers wanting to deter users attempt to dissuade consumers by pointing out the negative aspects. Shock advertising, price increases, restricted supply, government regulation of consuming a particular product and awareness programs can dampen consumption. Tobacco, illegal drugs and excessive consumption of alcohol are all targets for this type of marketing.

MARKETING MYOPIA

Marketing myopia arises when marketers lose sight of what is driving the consumer's purchasing decision: satisfying their needs. Marketing myopia occurs when the firm starts to market a product, not a solution to a need. In other words, they pay more attention to the product as a stand-alone object instead of highlighting the benefits and experiences a product offers a customer.

The current trouble with Microsoft's operating system is an excellent example of marketing myopia. Over the years, Windows has evolved from a simple point and click filing system to a interface that also allows users to do such diverse things as download and view images from digital cameras, play multimedia files, and communicate via instant messaging. Yet two problems that have plagued Microsoft's flagship product from its inception were stability and security. As more people become connected to the Internet, and the more computers automate critical services, the need for a secure and dependable operating system grows in kind. The spectacular collapse of computer networks around the world due to malicious viruses distributed reinforces an image of unreliability. Releasing the source code will improve the security and stability of Windows because instead of solely relying on Microsoft's software engineers to devise a patch, a worldwide pool of programmers would be constantly modifying the code to uncover strengths and weaknesses. Solutions and contingency plans would be devised well before issues become problems. However, due to Microsoft's continued recalcitrance to release the source code, more and more programmers, corporations, governments and even some home users are switching to an open-source operating system called Linux, which is not only free, but free for users to modify to how they see fit.

WHAT ARE THE RESPONSIBILITIES OF A MARKETING MANAGER?

Marketing is one of the central functions of a firm, the others typically being Research and Development, Manufacturing or Operations, Finance, IT, and HR. Whereas the other functions concentrate on internal matters, marketing's focus is solely on the customer. Marketing is the most critical of all activities for without a customer there is no revenue, leaving little for the other functions to do. As such, the fate of the organization rests in the abilities of its marketing managers.

It is difficult to generalize about the precise duties and responsibilities of marketing managers. The reason being if one were to do all of the activities that fall under the rubric of marketing, they'd be a communicator, seller, planner, researcher, analyst, product developer, supply chain specialist, or in other words, every activity that involves meeting a customer's need would be a responsibility of a marketing manager. A busy person indeed.

For the sake of that poor person who has to do everything, we've divided their tasks into five categories. The first would be to become market experts. Sales are the life and death of a company's fortunes. Understanding which market forces drive their respective market and how to stimulate demand using various tools and strategies is an essential skill. Secondly, a marketing manager is a communicator. They interact with customers to inform them about the benefits a product offers. Everything from advertisements to the labelling on the package sends a message to the customer of the benefits that reside within. At the same time, the marketing manager listens to customers to understand which needs are not being satisfied. In the long-term it is the customer who drives market dynamics. Third, a marketing manager is a steward. Brands are the bread and butter of companies. It is up to the marketing manager to oversee the program that strengthens and enhances the image of the brand. Forth, a marketing manager is also a negotiator. Rarely do producers sell directly to their customers. Instead they rely on intermediaries to distribute their product. Marketing managers need to learn how to negotiate deals with intermediaries that are beneficial to both parties. Finally, marketing managers are managers. They have face-to-face contact with other members of the organization; they oversee projects and rely on their personal values to help them through ethically difficult situations. Even when the job is simplified, a marketing manager needs to wear many hats.

MARKETING ORIENTATIONS

Businesses exist to make profit. They do so by selling products to consumers who seek to satiate unsatisfied needs. Given the variety of the products available, it should come as no surprise that there are many ways to market a product. We will now discuss the various marketing orientations companies use to sell to customers.

THE PRODUCTION CONCEPT

The production concept is a philosophy that states consumers will choose products that are affordable and widely available. Companies that adopt the product concept, focus their efforts on maximizing the available economies of scale. This focus entails improving the efficiency of production and distribution lines.

This strategy succeeds if two conditions are met: The manufacturer is not the distributor and market demand exceeds supply. The shortage pushes prices higher at the retail level, providing the manufacturer with an incentive to increase operational efficiencies or expand their operations should the excess demand persist.

The production concept is also applicable in situations where the price exceeds what the targeted market is willing to pay. Most people desire cars that minimize the amount of pollutants emitted into the air. However, not everyone can afford the $60,000 price tag. If production costs are lower, the price of the car will follow in tandem.

Firms using the production concept run the risk of succumbing to marketing myopia if by continually focusing on improving their operations internally they start to neglect the real objective of selling, which is to satisfy their customer's needs.

THE PRODUCT CONCEPT

Firms adopting the product concept believe consumers favour products that offer the most value after considering the quality, and performance of the product. This belief causes firms to continually improve their product. However, the product concept can lead to marketing myopia if the product becomes over-engineered. Cellphone manufacturers of the 3G cellular telephones were certain consumers would want to buy a phone that could be used anywhere in the world. It was only when features designed to enhance a user's individuality were added did sales take off.

THE SELLING CONCEPT

Firms implementing the selling concept believe consumers will buy a product only if the product is aggressively promoted. This concept is typically employed by companies that want to sell a product most people would not consider buying under normal circumstances. Companies that offer their products on infomercials are a good example of businesses that employ the selling concept.

Companies operating with the selling concept aim to sell products they believe the consumer wants, not making products the consumer needs. An unfortunate consequence of the selling concept approach is that it leads the business to believe consumers are easily manipulated by advertising.

Research has shown that companies with short-term minded orientations are not as profitable as those that seek to build long-term relationships by continually satisfying with a mindset to satisfy customer needs. Market forces eventually eliminate the "sell now before they figure it out" companies.

THE MARKETING CONCEPT

The marketing concept holds that companies must determine the needs of their consumers, and offers the product in a more efficient and superior manner than the competition. To effectively employ the marketing concept, there must be a well-defined market already in existence and the needs of the customer must be well defined. All operations of the business are directed to creating and delivering the desired product. The marketing approach creates a symbiotic relationship between consumers and suppliers, where businesses tie their survival to their customers, and their customers are bound to the company to satisfy their needs. Loyalty and trust form the basis of the relationship.

When the market is ill-defined or the customer is unsure of what their needs are, a situation arising from a lack of under-standing of a technology's potential, the firm must take the lead in the relationship by offering products they think the customer needs. Once the product is introduced, a market will emerge, and therein the firm starts communicating with their clients, whose participation directly influences the evolution of the product. Companies in high-technology industries are often in this situa-tion. When Sony introduced the Minidisc in the 1990s, users could record sound in a digital standard, but could download only using an analog signal in real time. At first, users didn't mind the incon-venience because digital recording equipment was very expensive. As more users started to use the minidisc as a stand-alone Walkman, Sony made their players MP3 compatible, allowing users to download music from their computers over a USB wire, and record in a variety of formats.

THE SOCIETAL MARKETING CONCEPT

The Societal Marketing Concept, or SMC as it is called is the newest of the marketing philosophies. It emerged from a realization that the marketing concept introduces conflicts between a consumer's short-term wants and their long-term welfare. The marketing concept drives companies to create long-term relation-ships with their customers; however, due to the compensation structure for executives, many incentives exist to direct the firm's energies to maximize the short-term value of the company's stock. Maximizing the short-term value of a company will not only undermine the long-term health of a company, but can also cause long-term harm to society and the consumer. Consider the fast-food industry for example. To deliver reasonably priced, tasty fast foods, fast-food companies have demanded farmers reduce the price per pound for beef. In order to meet this request, farmers are expanding their operations and implanting their livestock with growth-hormones. Though the cost savings are passed to consumers, society pays a heavy price. In Brazil, the expansion of cattle farms has increased the rate of clear-cutting the rainforest. Biodiversity is reduced, the risk of flooding in the region increases and as trees play an important role in converting carbon dioxide into oxygen, the rate of global warming increases. Now this might sound a bit over the top, but there is far too much evidence linking commercial activity to societal issues. Society pays the heavy price through the loss of biodiversity, increased acid rain, and there is evidence linking growth hormones to a variety of human diseases.

The SMC attempts to alleviate the conflict by adopting the premise that organizations should offer products that meet consumer need, in a more effective and efficient manner than their competitors while also maintaining or improving thw welfare of society. Since the SMC is a relatively new idea in marketing, it is still too early to tell how successful companies will be if they adopt the SMC approach over others. That said, Subway, a company that successfully marketed their food as part of a tasty weight-loss plan became North Americas largest fast-food chain in 2001.

Up to now, we've talked exclusively about products. But a product is classified either as a good or service. A good is any tangible object that has been manufactured, mined or harvested. Services are everything else. It might come as a surprise, but most economic activity in developed economies arises from the service industry. In the UK, manufacturing, mining and agricultural activity amounts to 30% of its **gross domestic product**, the *highest* level of the seven leading industrial nations. Collectively the seven produce in excess of $25 trillion of products. But most of the world's wealth is created from products that do not exist.

Though wealth creation is an exploration in metaphysics, there is a much more pressing problem.

The current practice of marketing is designed to promote consumerism. While consumerist-based societies offer a diverse set of choices, it also creates enormous amounts of waste, which contributes to the destruction of the planet. Corporate leaders are aware of the problem, and are trying to find ways to balance profit and socially responsible behaviour. However, the most effective way to enact change is not to expect our business leaders to lead the cause. Businesses respond to market signals, and therefore, it is up to the politicians and consumers to send the right messages. Stricter enforcement of environmental regulations, and changes in consumer behaviour would go a long way to improving all of our social welfare.

CONCLUSION

Marketing is the process of determining the consumer's needs and transferring that knowledge to the firm allowing for the appropriate product to be developed.

In the next chapter we will start to investigate how communication between the two parties takes place and how firms are building long-term relationships.

SUMMARY

- Marketing has two aims: Attracts new customers, and retains them by offering products satisfying other needs and wants.
- The fundamental principle underlying marketing theory is that humans experience periods of deprivation. This sense is caused by an instinctual behaviour to satisfy their intrinsic needs.
- Marketing myopia occurs when marketers lose sight of what the consumer needs.
- Products must be targeted to particular segments and attempts must be made to retain these customers.
- Marketers must also learn how to recognize and manage their product through different states of demand.
- There are many ways to market a product, some strategies are better than others. A company must balance short-term profit with long-term sustainability.

CRITICAL QUESTIONS

1   What is marketing and what are its fundamental concepts?
2   Compare and contrast the five marketing management orientations, paying close attention to word of mouth marketing.
3   Make a list of products you use every day, place them into their respective demand category. What would you do to market this product? Does it need to be relaunched?
4   Define marketing myopia and think of companies that might be suffering from it (here is a hint: Gillette).

SUGGESTIONS FOR FURTHER READING

Jakki Mohr, Sanjit Sengupta, and Stanley Slater, *Marketing of High-Technology Products and Innovations*, 2nd edition, New York, Prentice Hall, 2005.

There are not many good books on high-tech marketing; this is one of them. It presents key ideas for high-tech marketing in an understandable manner. Jakkie worked in the industry, for HP, for a number of years and it shows.

Philip Kotler and Kevin Lane Keller, *Marketing Management*, 12th edition, New Jersey, Prentice Hall, 2005.

Probably the best selling marketing textbook in the world are ones by Philip Kotler and his various co-authors. This is the US edition which I have used when I have taught in California and Hawaii. At McGill I use the Canadian edition, but there are editions for many other countries. It is a classic which is very regularly updated.

GLOSSARY

Behavioural segmentation   Dividing a market into groups based on the benefit sought.
Cognitive dissonance   The discomfort felt by a person when faced with choices that contradict the individual's personal values, beliefs or attitudes. This conflict drives the individual to select the option that minimizes the tension.

Demand A call or need for a particular product the consumer desires to satisfy their needs.

Demographics segmentation Dividing a target market on the basis of social identifiers, such as age, family size, income, gender, education, occupation, religion, social class etc.

Differentiation An activity that emphasizes the differences between products.

Gross domestic product The national production of a country in a year including exports.

Human needs Instinctual urges that must be satisfied. They include physical, social or individual.

Human wants The items humans decide to consume to satisfy a need given their culture and personality.

Market segmentation The process of dividing a population into distinct groups.

Marketing management The administering of the process of satisfying consumer needs while ensuring the company makes a profit.

Marketing mix The types of marketing strategies employed to meet an organization's objectives.

Marketing myopia When marketers lose sight of the fact that satisfying needs is driving the consumer's purchasing decision.

Psychographic segmentation Dividing a market into different groups based on attitudes, personal values, lifestyles or personalities.

Segment A group of customers that share one or many attributes with one another.

Target market The group the firm decides to market their product to.

Word of mouth When a customer shares their experience of a product with another.

2

MARKETING AS A CORPORATE FUNCTION

Marketing is one of the central functions of a firm, the others typically being, Research and Development, Manufacturing or Operations, Finance, IT, and HR. Whereas the other functions concentrate on internal matters, marketing's focus is solely the customer. Marketing is the most critical of all activities for without a customer there is no revenue, leaving little for the other functions to do. In the last chapter, we stressed the importance of adopting a marketing orientation. By creating goods that cater to the needs of the target market, a company creates a loyal customer base. Successfully implementing a customer-centric philosophy requires coordination among all levels of the organization. For small sized companies, it is possible to align the company's resources to meeting the target market's needs without a formal plan. For large sized companies, it is impossible. Large, diversified companies sell a variety of goods in an equally diverse set of industries to a diverse group of customers. To become more customer focused, large companies divide the organization into smaller units to decentralize managerial control: at the top there is the corporate unit, followed by the business unit and lastly the product unit. In this chapter we take a look at how marketing fits into the overall firm's strategy, and the decisions managers at the corporate and business unit level make in order to achieve those goals. Chapters three through five explore the issues managers face at the product unit level.

THE STRATEGIC PLAN

To ameliorate the inherent tensions between each organizational unit, and thereby create a strategy for the long-term, senior managers engage in a process called **strategic planning**. Strategic planning is a process of developing and maintaining a plan of action that coordinates the activities of every business unit to ensure the long-term goals of an organization are fulfilled. Over the course of a strategic planning session, a **strategic plan** emerges. The strategic plan is both a sermon and a pulpit. It clearly states the company's goals, and explains the sequence of events in how they will achieve their objectives. Once the strategic direction is set it is up to the various units to figure out how to creatively deliver the required results.

THE MISSION STATEMENT

A strategic plan starts with a **mission statement**. The mission statement explains in general terms the organization's goals and their *raison d'etre* or purpose. For example, here is the mission statement of Skype, a vendor of phone services that routes phone calls over the Internet:

> Skype aims to delight you by offering free global telephony, to make unlimited, superior quality voice calls via its next-generation peer-to-peer software. Skype's mission is providing a simple, reliable and friendly communications tool that just works. We aim for people to communicate with friends, families, and colleagues more flexibly, more cost effectively, and with better sound quality than ever previously imagined.

Studies have shown that well-crafted mission statements have three characteristics. They first focus on a limited number of goals that are challenging yet realistic. Second, mission statements explain the policies and values of the company. Third, they state which markets the company is targeting. Do you think managers at Skype have crafted such a mission statement?

CORPORATE STRATEGY

Typically, corporate strategy is crafted in a hierarchical fashion. Managers at the highest levels of the organization craft corporate strategies that take into account the structure of the industry (or industries) they operate within and the companies they compete against. The managers at the business unit level develop the strategies to achieve the goals and provide guidelines and profit targets to managers at the product level, who develop and implement the programs to meet the overall corporate objectives.

THE CORPORATE STRATEGIC PLAN

The aim of the corporate plan is to provide managers at every level of the organization with a framework which captures the current state of the market(s) they operate within.

BUSINESS CYCLES

In helping to build your corporate and business strategy going forward you need to understand the bigger economic picture. Knowing where you and your customers are in the business cycle is important. One of the features of a market economy is that if you plot the growth of output over a long period of time, what emerges is a graph that is marked by periods of relatively rapid growth followed by a period of decline of output. While these peaks and valleys can persist for years, the average of these values would be positive. A **business cycle** is the time between peak-to-peak or valley-to-valley. Some key indicators of the state of the economy include increases in productivity, consumer confidence, **gross domestic product** (GDP) and employment levels. Assuming your company's fortunes are closely tied to the state of the economy, the more positive news relative to the past suggests the market would be receptive to growth strategies. If the news was pessimistic, a cautious approach is appropriate.

Beyond the bigger macroeconomic picture it is very helpful to understand the industry you are competing in and its dynamics. One of the most popular models of understanding your firm's industry is the Five Forces Model devised by Harvard Business Professor Michael Porter. His model suggests the user consider five key factors or forces: 1) *Barriers to Entry* or how hard it is to enter the market. An example of a barrier to entry in the high-tech industry might be a proprietary standard such as Microsoft's Windows® operating system. 2) *Degree of Rivalry* in the industry or how many firms are competing for the pie. The more players going after the same market typically means lower prices and hence lower profitability. 3) The *Power of Suppliers,* how much power do your suppliers have over your firm. If you need aluminium to make your product and the price goes up because of growing demand from China you will find it harder to bargain with Alcan or Alcoa. 4) The *Power of Buyers,* how much power does your buyers have over you. The automotive industry has dramatically reduced the number of parts suppliers they have used, the result is that Ford and the other big players have severely squeezed auto parts manufacturers profits. Finally, 5) the *Threat of Substitutes,* or if your price goes too high do your customers have real alternatives that they could move to? For example if the price of petrol goes up wind power and solar power become more viable alternatives of energy sources.

BUSINESS UNIT CORPORATE STRATEGY

Once the corporate strategy plan has been established, the next stage of the strategic plan is to create the business unit corporate strategy. Many large sized companies organize their business units into semi-autonomous units called **strategic business units (SBU)**. SBUs are given nearly full autonomy to conduct their affairs because they are closer to the customer and are more likely to respond quickly to changes in the market than a more centralized company. Each strategic business unit develops strategies tailored to fit their resources and capabilities to fulfil the overall corporate objective outlined by senior management.

SBUs develop and harness their **core competencies**. A core competency is a task, skill or resource that enables a company to have an advantage over their competitors. A core competency has the following three characteristics:

- difficult to imitate;
- potentially opens access to a wide variety of markets;
- increases perceived customer benefits.

Management professors C. K. Prahalad and Gary Hamel first introduced the concept of core competencies in 1990. They argue that firms should carefully consider the historical success of their firm to understand what they are world-class at and use these experiences, abilities or competencies as a launching pad for future products and market forays. An example they cite is Japanese automotive giant Honda. One of their core competencies is manufacturing high quality yet inexpensive engines. By tweaking the design, Honda was able to exploit their core competency in engine manufacturing, to move into other product categories that also used motorized engines such as lawn mowers, motorcycles and snow blowers – categories of product which did not very often share the same customers. By harnessing core competencies, a company can leap into seemingly distant product categories.

Core competencies that endure over a long period of time create a **sustained competitive advantage**. They called the plane the 747. When they introduced the plane in 1970, it was the only long-distance aircraft manufacturer that could carry over 450 passengers. For another company to build a suitable alternative, they would have to have invested billions in research and development. Until various European governments agreed to use taxpayer funds to create Airbus, Boeing was the only company that could build cost-effective long-haul aeroplanes. Their virtual monopoly lasted almost 35 years.

ASSIGNING RESOURCES TO SBUS

As we mentioned earlier, senior management devises a corporate strategic plan and assigns resources to each SBU taking into account the state of the economy. When it comes to allocating resources, managers must contend with the problem of scarcity. To overcome this problem, SBUs are evaluated in a similar manner to how one would evaluate their investment portfolio. However there is a twist. When evaluating one's personal investments, the majority of funds are placed in high performing assets, and some funds are diverted to safe investments to offset the risk. When it comes to allocating resources to SBUs a problem emerges. An investor can easily liquidate a bad investment. Business assets cannot be dispensed as quickly. One wrong move ties up resources for a long time. Managers need a tool to help them make informed decisions with respect to allocating resources.

THE BCG APPROACH

One popular tool is called the BCG Approach. This model was developed by the Boston Consulting Company in the 1970s. Their model assesses the performance of SBUs according to their relative market share and the growth rate (see Figure 2.1). The relative market share indicates the SBU's market share relative to their largest competitor. The closer the relative market share is to the point of origin on the map, the larger the relative market share the SBU

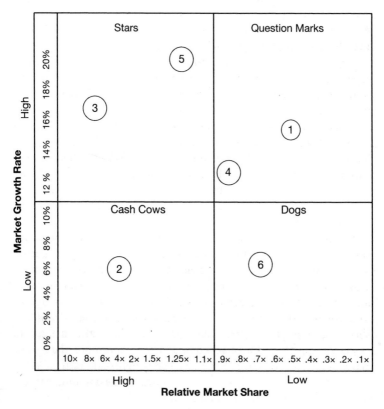

Figure 2.1   Boston Consulting Group (BCG) Growth-Share Matrix

controls. In other words, if a SBU controlled 25% of the market and their nearest competitor only controlled 5%, the SBU would have a relative market share of 5x.

The graph is divided into four cells, each representing a type of business. SBUs with high market share and high growth are called "stars"; the "cash cows" are SBUs with high market share but low growth; SBUs with low market share and low growth are called dogs. Finally, SBUs with growth rates but low market share are called "question marks".

Using the BCG technique, managers quickly assess which SBUs are growing rapidly (stars), which SBUs could be milked to finance the growth (cash cows), and which SBUs to divest (dogs). Question marks have the potential of being turned into stars, but they require development through increased funding and resources. With this model, managers can create a pecking order as to who receives funding first.

Besides being used as a tool to allocate funding to SBUs, companies use the model to aide in product-line decisions. Cellphone manufacturer Ericsson for example, plots the market performance of their 2G and 3G product-lines. Over time, the 2G phones moved from being a star to a cash cow and eventually a dog. Doing this allows them to change funding levels by timing critical decisions better. However, when analysing at a product level, the manager mustn't make the mistake of assuming all markets are alike. As we said earlier, products are technology driven, markets are time driven. If a product is a dog in one market, it could still be a cash cow in another.

Models such as the BCG approach have its fair share of critics. They contend that using such an approach tempts managers to believe that using a simple and elegant model solves all of the problems related to resource allocation. Furthermore, it assumes SBUs are completely independent entities. In practice that is rarely the case. SBUs share resources, capabilities, personnel and facilities. Divesting dogs that offer synergies introduces the danger of adversely affecting well performing SBUs. Furthermore, the results of the model are sensitive to the assigned weights and ratings. What market you compete in is not often as clear-cut as one might think. How you define the market can dramatically affect your market share. Coke is doing well against Pepsi for share of the market but compared to water (another key competitor) it has a very low market share. Also, the results can be manipulated to create a desirable outcome. On a practical level it is often demoralizing for a business unit to realize that they are just a cow – merely fit to spin off their profit to support more "sexy" products. In fact if more of the profits which they produce were reinvested in their product it might actually have the potential for greater growth. Thus, too often, the model can be used to place far too much emphasis on promoting stars at the expense of cash cows.

THE PRODUCT LIFE-CYCLE

In biology, an organism's life can be divided into four stages: birth, growth, adulthood and decline. The sales curve of a product over time also exhibits the same characteristics, though marketers prefer to label the four stages as introduction, growth, maturity and decline. This sequence is known as the **product life-cycle**. Figure 2.2 illustrates a typical product life-cycle. On the horizontal axis is the length of time the product is on the market, while on the vertical axis is sales revenue. As the figure shows, typically revenue for a product follows an elongated "S" shape curve over its lifetime.

A product's "life" begins with its introduction to the marketplace. Sales volume is low, and losses are registered since all the costs associated with developing and bringing the product to market are borne. Resources are spent promoting the product to increase its visibility. This is most critical time in a product's life, most new products fail and die off early. The job of the marketer is clear, to work very hard to get the product past the critical early days and successfully to the growth stage.

At the heart of this effort is to understand how and why people adopt new products, services or ideas. In any population, whether it be as broad as Germans who drink beer to as narrow as dentists in Melbourne, most people don't like change and don't like to try new things. Thankfully for marketers there are exceptions. There is a small percentage, generally taken as about 2.5% whom are visionaries or innovators who are willing to try out a new thing without evidence that anyone else has; these are people who don't look around to see who else is using the new product but are willing to buy on their feelings and intuition. The next group is bigger, about

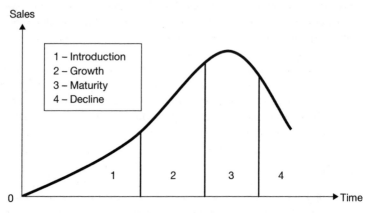

Figure 2.2 Product Life-cycle

13.5% of the population who are early adopters; next are the early majority (34%), late majority (34%) and finally laggards (16%) who will often adopt a new product many years after the innovators did. A key thought is that the early majority will adopt only after the early adopters because they must see a fair number of people already using the product before they are willing take on the risk of adopting it themselves. Thus we see that adoption is very much a social process. The late majority are again even more careful and will only adopt after they see a great number of people are using the product. This model works with products and services but also with ideas. New ideas, smoking is bad for example, take time to spread or diffuse across a population and a majority will accept them only after the early groups, the innovators and early adopters have first come to accept the new view.

Some of the characteristics of each category of adopter that have been suggested include:

- innovators – venturesome, educated, multiple info sources;
- early adopters – social leaders, popular, educated;
- early majority – deliberate, many informal social contacts;
- late majority – sceptical, traditional, lower socio-economic status;
- laggards – neighbours and friends are main info sources, fear of debt.

As more and more customers adopt the product, the product enters the growth stage. Here, sales revenue grows quickly, costs per unit decline, and profits increase because the product experiences positive economies of scale. Once sales of the product have peaked, the product enters a phase of maturity. Eventually customers' tastes change contributing to the product's *decline* and possible elimination from the marketplace altogether. The concepts we have been covering thus far in this chapter are firmly based in marketing today and will undoubtedly be useful for many years to come. In the next section we will turn to two key emerging areas in marketing. In some cases a product can enjoy what is called a "scalloped" life-cycle with new growth taking place during the decline stage bringing new life to a moribund product. Cow brand baking soda did this a few years ago. With fewer people baking at home, the sales of baking soda declined. A clever marketer breathed new life into sales by finding a new application, using an open box of baking soda to remove bad smells in a refrigerator. Though one suspects cleaning the refrigerator would do a better job, nevertheless many started adopting the product for this use.

THE EXPERIENTIAL ECONOMY

"The fox knows many things, but the hedgehog knows one big thing". There are few things we can say with confidence, or at least some confidence, about the future. One of those few for us is that we are in the midst of a massive move to an experience economy.

For much of the 19th century the west's economy was dominated by an extraction or commodities economy. Starting in the late 18th century the British started the Industrial Revolution and were the dominant manufacturing power during that century, though France, Germany and the US also had important parts to play. At its peak Britain was manufacturing over 50% of the finished products in world trade. Much of the rest of the world was left behind; even the US was still dominated by agriculture and other commodity businesses. Starting in the early 20th century but especially after World War II, manufacturing became more central.

Since the 1970s we have seen a dramatic shift to a services economy. According to the government statistics in the last decade the US/Canadian services sector now employs three out of four North

Americans and generates two-thirds of our gross domestic product. In North America there are effectively no new net manufacturing jobs being created. We are now in the midst of the next broad shift, however it is less obvious and subtler than the transformation from manufacturing to services. It is easy to say whether you are in manufacturing or services. Being firmly in the experience economy means that you are also part of the services economy. It is a change of attitude and outlook that differentiates an experience focused firm from a services firm. The thing which has forcibly struck us in the last year or two is that this is for almost every firm, not just for the top tier.

Staying at a Four Seasons Hotel, visiting Disneyland with the children, shopping at Tokyo's chic Takashimaya department store. Inarguably, all great experiences. But are they in a class by themselves? That is the lesson which we think has not fully sunk in for many marketers. Our belief is that virtually every firm must begin to think about how they will offer a substantial portion of their customer set an improved experience. Note, at this point, that only a portion will view your offering this way.

What we see in North America, Western Europe and Japan is a bifurcating of consumer behaviour. The same consumer is shopping at both Wal-Mart and Nordstrom's. On one hand, they want the cheap and cheerful offer of Wal-Mart for a substantial portion of their spending. Contrary to the past they also want to go upscale as they can for some selected items. We live more demanding, stressful, Blackberry, cellphone, email beeping interrupted lives. We want to be financially sensible in some lower involvement items but we also deserve some spoiling – we've earned it! This appears to be true across the board. Not just in the upper or middle income but also in lower income levels as well. For the, I-am, owed-it category of shoppers, experience is absolutely paramount. However, the fascinating thing is that it is also creeping into the other, more mundane, categories as well. Of course, which category your product fits into depends not so much on your product as on the individual shopper's view of it.

The challenge that marketers are facing who are not the Takashimaya or Four Seasons or Saks Fifth Avenues of the world is how do we integrate a great experience at a more sensible price point? Most simply cannot afford the almost over-the-top service, though wonderful if you can afford it, of a personal shopper at a top-of-the-line department store.

It is early days, however, some first or second efforts are suggesting it can be done. We have been doing some work with a high-tech giant in the US where as part of a two-day marketing seminar we do group work to figure out how to make the experience of buying a personal computer a superior one. This is a fairly mundane purchase, much of it done via phone, web and/or in a store. Yet the participants are able to come up with some quite innovative ways of enhancing the customer experience. Recently Canada's largest telephone company, Bell Canada, appointed a Vice President of Customer Experience and Air Canada similarly recently appointed a Vice President of In-flight Customer Experience, both fairly mundane, common, everyday purchases for many. Yet these large firms made key executive appointments to focus on the fact of their entry into the experience economy. On a more mundane level yet still, we can think of our local neighbourhood supermarket which is more expensive than when we make our weekly trek to a large box store for serious family food shopping. Yet, the pleasantness of the staff, the butcher remembering our favourite cut of beef, the harried talk with the fishmonger about farmed versus wild salmon, the chances of running into a neighbour and having a nice chat, in other words, the fun of shopping – the experience, keeps us coming back.

Our question to you is simple, what is your business doing to ensure that your customer's experience is a superior one to buying from you in the past and buying from your competition?

CONCLUSION

Companies need to become more customer focused. The emergence of an experience-based economy only serves to underscore the need, otherwise, the products sold will be classified as a low-involvement good by cost-conscious customers looking to save a buck to buy more luxuries. Products that compete solely on price face a race to the bottom. To avoid getting caught in a cost-trap, managers must make difficult decisions with regards to allocating resources to ensure customers continue to have a favourable impression of the product. Corporate planning plays a major role in this matter. The corporate plan outlines the objectives, and the

SBUs implement them. Over the next three chapters we will show you exactly how that is done.

SUMMARY

- Large sized organizations decentralize decision making powers to smaller organizational units to better respond to customer needs.
- To coordinate activities between SBUs, a strategic plan is created at the corporate level.
- Though the life-cycle of a product is "S" shaped over time, managers can delay a product's death by changing the marketing mix.
- The emergence of consumers who are at times seeking experience or thrift is radically changing the corporate landscape.

CRITICAL QUESTIONS

1   Take a look at Figure 2.1. If SBU#2 could only be milked to fuel one star SBU, which one should be chosen? If SBU#2 could be milked to fund every SBU, in what order should funding be allocated? Should the dogs be divested? In which circumstances should dogs be kept in the portfolio?

2   According to some studies, the number of children classi-fied as obese is well over 30%. Knowing that there are innovators, early adopters and other types of people, devise a list of strategies that you think would combat the problem of obesity. Next, assess which ideas are likely to diffuse into the general population? Is there a role for government to play in the equation? What can marketers do to help solve this social problem?

SUGGESTIONS FOR FURTHER READING

Geoffrey Moore, *Crossing the Chasm*, New York, Collins, 2002.

This is very well written book that talks about the adoption of innovations with a focus on the high-tech sector but with principles that we believe are applicable across the board for all marketers.

Malcolm Gladwell, *The Tipping Point*, New York, Back Bay Books, 2002.

An amazing, popular book and for good reason. It brings to life key issues around the adoption of innovation. Malcolm is a writer for the *New Yorker* magazine and writes in an engaging way.

GLOSSARY

Business cycle   The period of time consisting of alternating periods of growth and decline in terms of GDP.

Core Competency   A task, skill or resource that enables a company to have an advantage over their competitors.

Mission Statement   A summary of the stated goals of the organization.

Product life-cycle   The revenue of a product over its lifetime.

Strategic planning   A process of developing and maintaining a plan of action that coordinates the activities of every business unit to ensure the long-term goals of an organization are fulfilled.

Strategic Business Unit (SBU)   A semi-autonomous unit of a large sized company, often in charge of setting its own corporate strategy.

Strategic plan   The roadmap that outlines how the goals and objectives will be achieved.

Sustained Competitive Advantage   An enduring core competency that provides lucrative returns for a company over time.

3

PRODUCT AND PLACEMENT

Now that we have discussed in detail the role marketing plays in a firm's corporate strategy, we now turn our attention to the various elements of the marketing mix better known as the five Ps (product, place, price, promotion, people). Over the next three chapters we investigate how decisions about the product itself, its placement or how it is distributed to customers, the price charged, types of promotion used, and the people needed to support the product are all potential sources of competitive advantage.

PART A: PRODUCT

In marketing, a **product** is much more than just a physical object; it is a bundle of physical, psychological and experiential benefits that the customer receives that satisfies one or many wants or needs. Fully understanding the benefits a customer receives is no simple task. It requires insight on the logical and impulsive reasons why purchases are made.

CUSTOMER VALUE HIERARCHY THEORY

Researchers have debated at length the relationship between a product and customer value. One theory called the customer value hierarchy suggests representing the benefits a customer receives as a hierarchy of three levels (see Figure 3.1). The more levels to the product, the more value the customer receives.

The first level is called the **core benefit level**. At this level, customers purchase a product because of the functional benefit the product offers. For example, a person buys a television because they need information to make informed decisions and desire entertainment in an accessible manner. A television satisfies these requirements by transmitting content in the form of images.

Most products offer more than functional benefits. Customers evaluate how the product fares in delivering the core benefit. When a customer evaluates the **expected product level**, they take into account how the product's attributes, features, quality, styling, packaging, delivers the core benefit. Returning to our example about television screens, the customer takes into account such features as

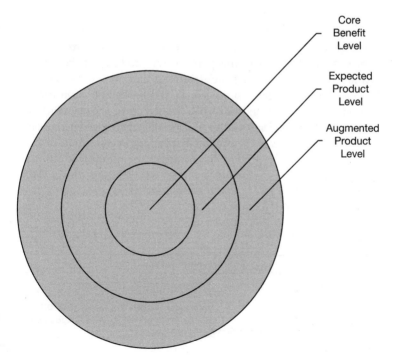

Core
Benefit
Level

Expected
Product
Level

Augmented
Product
Level

Figure 3.1 Model of Customer Value Hierarchy

size; shape – flat screen or curved; picture quality – plasma, LCD or cathode-ray tube; sound, and name of manufacturer. Combined, these features and qualities produce televised images.

After considering the core benefits and the ability of the product's features to deliver those benefits, products that offer auxiliary benefits offer an even higher level of value. At the **augmented product level**, customers consider the value they receive from a vendor's after-sales support, warranty, promise of free delivery or installation, credit availability, and technical support.

The customer value hierarchy theory provides a great deal of insight into how a product can be designed to build competitive advantage. In essence it claims customers seek products that satisfy their needs more conveniently, completely and cost-effectively. In other words, those products that offer the most value in the long run will be the most successful in their respective categories.

THE PRODUCT MIX

Most vendors sell more than one product in different product categories. Marketers define the portfolio of products offered to the market as the **product mix**. For classification purposes, the product mix is divided into four dimensions: length, width, depth and consistency. Consider the product-mix matrix of a fictitious beverage manufacturer.

The **product-line length** is the number of products sold in one category. For this company the product-line length in soft drinks product category is four. The **product-line width** is the number of different categories the company operates within, which in this case is three. **Product-line depth** refers to the number of varying packaging sizes

Table 3.1 Product-Mix Matrix of a Fictitious Beverage Company

	Product-Line Width		
	Soft Drinks	Bottled Water	Juices
Product-Line Length	Generic Cola Ripe Lemon-Lime Vanilla-Flavoured Cola Ripe Orange Surprise	Tastes like Tap Water Glacial-like Ice Eau de la Spring	100% ripe orange 100% ripe apple

of each product. Suppose our company sells Generic Cola brand in "Take a Big Gulp", "Leaves You Wanting More" and "I'm on a Diet" serving sizes. The product-line depth for Generic Cola would be three. Finally, **product-line consistency** assesses how correlated, or closely related, each product-line is to each other in terms of benefits they offer consumers. In our example, the product-line is consistency high because all of their product-lines are designed to quench one's thirst.

The purpose of assigning numerical values to the product-line, length, depth and consistency is to create a matrix or table of a firm's portfolio. The matrix in turn provides a platform in which to evaluate the performance of a dimension in relation to another dimension, or in relation to the entire portfolio. To conduct this analysis, managers must assess the performance of each product within each dimension. These tests indicate which products need to be built, maintained, harvested or divested in order to meet the corporate objective. Below are some tests managers use to determine performance at the product level.

INVENTORY TURNOVER

The inventory turnover rate is a measure of the number of times a company's inventory is replaced during a given time period. Turnover ratio is calculated as cost of goods sold divided by average inventory during the time period. A high turnover ratio is a sign that the company is producing and selling its goods or services very quickly. Most distributors who have 20%–30% gross margins strive to achieve an overall turnover rate of five to six turns per year. One of the secrets to Dell's success versus its former competitor Compaq (now part of high-tech giant HP) is that Dell had twice the inventory turnover as Compaq.

RETURN ON INVESTMENT (ROI)

ROI is a very common tool used to measure the return on an investment. It is calculated using the following formula:

$$ROI = \frac{V_f}{V_i} - 1$$

where V_i is the initial investment and V_f is the final value.

When calculating ROI, a firm tries to incorporate all costs associated with making the product. Positive ROI means the product is creating shareholder value. ROI is one of the most popular tools used by managers today because of the powerful conclusions one can make using a simple formula.

Interestingly, the above formula misleads how much value was destroyed if an investment soured. Let us suppose the initial investment was $100 and the investment yielded a 10% return. That would result in an overall return of $110. However, if the same investment yielded a return of -10%, the return would be $99 not $90 as expected.

RETURN ON CAPITAL (ROC)

Return on capital is also known as Return On Invested Capital (ROIC). It is defined as the net income on an investment divided by the capital invested in the project. Some managers include borrowing costs in their calculation of ROC. When the ROC is higher than the company's **cost of capital**, then the company is creating value to the shareholders.

PRODUCT LEVEL STRATEGIES

Having discussed some of the tests managers use to assess the performance of a product, these numbers need to be placed within a corporate strategy perspective. The numbers can declare if a product is performing exceptionally, however, if that product is succeeding in a mature market, those results are likely to be attributed to other players exiting the market. To succeed in the long-term, the company must change their product mix over time. The next section discusses a number of strategies at a firm's disposal to change the product mix. For many firms they have rules of thumb that a certain percentage (say 50%) of sales must come from products less than 5 years in the market, in high-tech markets they would often use a benchmark of 2 years rather than 5 years.

PRODUCT-FILLING

Product-filling is a strategy whereby the vendor offers the same products in different shapes, sizes, qualities or prices. The aim is to capture as much of the consumer surplus as possible by customizing the offering to different buyers with the same needs and wants. Pharmaceutical companies frequently stretch their product-line to capture market share. For example, for each brand of painkillers they offer, users can purchase a product of varying strength, method of consumption (pill or gel-cap), and length of effectiveness.

By offering a wide variety of products under one brand, product-lining offers a low-cost, low-risk way to meet unsatisfied buyer needs. What's more, by extending a product-line, the vendor's bargaining power with retailers increases because the vendor accounts for a higher percentage of the retailer's total sales. Other strategic advantages include blocking entry opportunities for competitors, raising the entry price for competitors, and utilizing excess capacity. From a competitive perspective, product-filling poses a real problem. Smaller firms and foreign firms trying to break into the shelves of large retailers cannot do so because the shelves are dominated by existing competitors.

Line-filling can be detrimental to a business as well. By offering more items in a product-line, the practice could result in **self-cannibalization**. Self-cannibalization is the reduction in volume, revenue or market share of one product as a result of the introduction of another product by the same producer. Some analysts believe the introduction of the iPod Mini will hurt future profits at Apple.

LINE-STRETCHING

Line-stretching entails lengthening the product-line by offering products to potential customers residing upstream and/or downstream. Firms engage in line-stretching because they are striving to become a full-line vendor, they are chasing higher margins or growth or they are doing so for tactical reasons. The aim of line-stretching is to create a product-line that meets every unmet need subject to the firm's goals and resources.

Typically, firms engage in an **upstream stretch** to grab market share in higher margin, but lower volume markets. The Honda Acura and Lexus are two examples of middle-market car manufacturers trying to steal market share in the premium sector of the automobile industry. In come cases, moving a product upstream creates a premium market in a product category. Coffee and ice cream were always regarded as commodity style markets. Yet, Starbucks and Haagen Daaz deliberately priced their product considerably higher than their competitors, choosing instead to compete on quality and experience.

A **downstream stretch** is employed either for growth or tactical reasons. By moving downstream a company positioned in the middle-market increases their inventory turnover. This in turn utilizes excess capacity and increases the pace it takes to ride the **learning curve**. Moving downstream is also a defensive strategy. By moving downstream, the higher end marketer attacks lower-end competitors in their primary markets.

Finally, a **two-way stretch** is where companies serving the middle-market decide to stretch their product-line in both directions. An example is Marriott hotels which stretched upscale with their purchase of the Ritz-Carlton chain and then downscale with three other brands, Resident Inn and Courtyard and Fairfield Inn. For example, Residence Inn targets those who are looking for a "home away from home" for travellers staying 5 nights or more. Features include things which appeal to this segment: complimentary hot breakfast, evening hospitality hour, swimming pool, sport court, personalized grocery shopping, guest suites with separate living and sleeping areas and a fully equipped kitchen.

PRODUCT-LINE PRUNING

Researchers have observed that product-lines tend to lengthen over time. Growth targets, excess capacity, and the strategic importance of offering a complete range of products to satisfy all of the customer's needs are often the reasons for expanding the product-line. While lengthening the product-line meets growth targets, adding more products also adds administrative, promotional, production, labour, and research costs. What's more cannibalization issues also need to be considered. Managers must routinely review the profitability of each product, and prune those that are not sources of competitive advantage. In the high technology industry cannibalization often occurs when a firm announces a new product early. Microsoft and IBM have both done this in recent years; there is even a name for it, vapourware, in contrast to hardware and software. By pre-announcing a product before it is ready for the market the firm effectively "shoots itself in the foot", because sales of its own existing products often dramatically decline. Firms do this in order to pre-empt consumers from buying a competitor's product.

Products that offer the most value are the most successful products in their respective categories. Managers must find a balance between strategic and financial considerations to ensure the product mix offered to customers does in fact offer the highest value possible. Over time, customer preferences change, and as such, changes at the expected product level and augmented product level must be made periodically. Furthermore, for multi-product vendors, the product portfolio must be reviewed periodically to ensure every product offered is providing a higher value added return to shareholders.

PART B: PLACEMENT

The second element of the marketing mix is called placement. Manufacturers rarely sell directly to their customers. Instead, they sell their product through one or more **marketing channels**. Sometimes called a channel of distribution or trade channel, marketing channels are defined by the American Marketing Association as "an organized network of agencies and institutions which, in combination, perform all the functions required to link producers with end customers to accomplish the marketing task". A marketing channel is a group of interdependent organizations involved in the process of production and distribution of a good or service.

Developing the right marketing channel to reach a target market is crucial to the success of a product. As E. Raymond Corey notes:

> A distribution channel system is a key external resource. Normally it takes years to build and it is not easily changed. It ranks in importance with key internal resources such as manufacturing, research, engineering and field-salespersonnel and facilities. It represents a significant corporate commitment to large numbers of independent companies whose business is distribution – and to the particular markets they

serve. It represents, as well, a commitment to a set of policies and practices that constitute the basic fabric on which is woven an extensive set of long-term relationships.

The implications of deciding which marketing channel to use are clear and once a distribution system is established, it cannot be changed easily. However, if the right channels are chosen, the distribution system becomes a source of competitive advantage because the seller has privileged access to their target markets.

For the remainder of this chapter, we inspect the ins and outs of placement. We will illustrate the need for intermediaries, their role in the exchange process and how to manage the relationship between manufacturers and intermediaries. We then show how a manufacturer creates a marketing channel, analyse the relationship between the manufacturer and its intermediaries and how to manage the marketing channel.

THE SUPPLY CHAIN VIEWED AS A VALUE NETWORK

Before we begin our discussion, we must take a step back and address a few issues regarding the **supply chain**. Traditionally, the supply chain has been regarded as a linear process: raw materials are extracted and refined, then sent to a manufacturing plant where it is machined into a product, then the product is either sold to the consumer directly or through a series of intermediaries. In this "make and sell" perspective, there is little to no coordination in the supply chain between members that are not adjacent to each other in the process. Coordinating structural, technological, contractual and behavioural issues in the entire system is problematic to say the least. Because of such difficulties, historically, product offerings were not built according to customer need, but rather on maximizing short-term profits based on the production or distribution capabilities of the upstream and downstream parties.

Marketers believe that a linear supply chain perspective should be bent into a shape more reflective of the business environment. Conceptually, regarding the supply chain as a process in which a resource undergoes a series of transformations is true, but such a perspective fails to capture the underlying dynamics driving the system. Business processes are better represented by flows of information, cash, people, and physical products moving in, out and between the various members of the marketing channel. These flows create complex behavioural systems, which in turn affect individuals, departments, companies, and even economies.

Customer value is created when the needs and wants of the customer are satisfied. Those firms that create partnerships to best align these flows to improve the performance of the system, create what is known as a **value network**. Value networks are more efficient than linear supply chains because every aspect of the system is aligned to the purpose of creating customer value, not maximizing short-term profit.

THE VALUE NETWORK

A value network is a system of interdependent organizations needed to source, support, and deliver a product that provides customers with the highest level of value. Upstream, suppliers offer value by guaranteeing the quality and time of delivery of the product. Downstream, intermediaries act as marketing channels to the targeted customer. A value network offers many advantages. The first is that it increases specialization. Since each company is guaranteed a source of supply, each firm can concentrate on those activities which they do best. The second advantage is that it allows every member of the network to become aware of disturbances in the supply chain much more quickly. If problems arise upstream or downstream, all members of the network are affected, a considerable incentive to ensure cooperation is used to resolve the problem. Finally, a value network increases the likelihood that firms will integrate certain parts of their operations with adjacent partners to ensure the network is operating smoothly. A well-managed and properly designed value network decreases cost and increases efficiency. What's more, by orienting a firm's operations to maximizing customer value the firm in turn becomes better at "sensing and responding to" customers needs.

An example of a value network is Airbus and the way it is manufacturing the giant 555 passenger A 380. Airbus has chosen a number of what are called Tier I producers, which they use to supply key modules and sub-assemblies to Airbus. Airbus then assembles the behemoth in Toulouse, France. Among their many Tier 1 suppliers are TRW for Aileron and Rudder, Rockwell Collins for Avionics, FMS for Cockpit Systems, and Pratt and Whitney for the Auxiliary Power Unit, suppliers from both Europe and North America in this case. Tier II suppliers would be supply these suppliers with parts and sub-modules in tern.

MARKETING CHANNELS

As we said earlier, choosing the channels to market is vitally important in business. Once established, a marketing channel is almost mollified. Given the stakes involved as a consequence of globalization, the question arises why would a manufacturer, particularly a large sized one, trust intermediaries to bring their product to market? Surely developing a well-functioning marketing channel is difficult, but not impossible.

Louis W. Stern and Adel I. El-Ansary offer a useful explanation as to why a producer would rely on an intermediary:

> Intermediaries smooth the flow of goods and services . . . This procedure is necessary in order to bridge the discrepancy between the assortment of goods and services generated by the producer and the assortment of demanded by the consumer. The discrepancy results from the fact that manufacturers typically produce a large quantity of a limited variety of goods, whereas consumers usually desire only a limited quantity of a wide variety of goods.

Consumers want convenience and variety. The cost to reach a critical mass of customers is simply too high to justify creating a proprietary channel for most manufacturers. By specializing, producers can concentrate on activities they're best at, which is designing, developing and manufacturing their product. Shifting the responsibilities of distribution and selling, which requires competencies in logistics, warehousing, information gathering, and a network of sales agents, is in the interest of the manufacturer with production competencies. Efficiency increases; production costs decreases. It is these two factors that provide economic incentives for manufacturers to create relationships with intermediaries. Intermediaries add customer value.

CHANNEL LEVELS

Preventing the producer from realizing a sale are the marketing channels the product must traverse through before it reaches the consumer. Some products require no intermediaries; others require multiple ones.

A zero-level channel is one where the producer is the distributor. Mail order, and companies that sell their products on the Internet have a zero-level channel; Dell is a great example of a company successfully in doing this. ICE.com is another example; this online only firm sells jewellery from Montreal around world with the US and the UK as the dominant markets. They believe that other markets will become more active as they get more experience buying online.

A one-level channel is where there is one intermediary, most often a retailer, between the customer and producer. A two-level channel is where there are two intermediaries, and so on and so on. The number of intermediaries profoundly affects how a product is marketed. The more intermediaries means the less responsibilities – and less cost – the manufacturer incurs. However, by outsourcing control to other partners, the producer has less influence in how the product is marketed and distributed. There needs to be a balance between lowering production cost and controlling marketing. When Wal-Mart entered Canada in the early 90s the number of intermediaries in the Canadian retailing market declined from 5 to 4. Wal-Mart was simply more efficient and their involvement in the Canadian marketplace meant that other retailers had to increase their efficiency; one way was by reducing the number of channel members by one on average.

CHANNEL ORGANIZATION

We said earlier that changing the placement strategy is much more difficult than changing the price or promotion strategy. While the process of distribution is quite static, the players within the system are not; the dynamics within the marketing channel are surprisingly fluid. New types of intermediaries emerge; mergers, bankruptcies and changing market conditions mean channel systems never stand still. Because there is a constant uncertainty within the distribution system, in order for the entire system to work effectively, a leader is needed to assign roles and manage disputes between partners. In the next section, we take a closer look at three types of marketing channels that provide the needed leadership to assign roles and manage disputes.

VERTICAL MARKETING CHANNELS

The first type of marketing channel that provides the necessary leadership to assign roles and manage disputes is called a vertical marketing channel. In this system, a set of producers, wholesalers, and retailers act in concert to maximize the returns for the collective. In this system, channel members engage in a practice called **cross-ownership**, each member of the channel owns a percentage of the other partner's companies. If cross-ownership is not possible, or is illegal, contracts can be devised that bind the companies together, or if the market power of one company is so great, all members of the system must cooperate for fear of losing the contract. Wal-Mart is an example of a company whose buying power is so high that the threat of exclusion is sufficient enough to coerce suppliers to cooperate. In a vertical marketing channel system, the firm that assigns roles and manages conflict can be a producer, wholesaler or retailer. The Japanese economy serves as a cautionary tale on the drawbacks of vertical marketing channels. Most of the Japanese economy has been organized in this manner, the difference being that the lending institution (typically a bank) also owns shares in each company in the vertical marketing channel. Following the bursting of a real-estate bubble, economic growth has been virtually stagnant for the last 15 years. One of the reasons the economy remains in the doldrums is because some of the banks that have extensive holdings in other companies are insolvent. If the bank collapses, it takes all of its partners with it.

HORIZONTAL MARKETING CHANNELS

A horizontal marketing channel system is where firms at the same level of the channel form a joint venture to pursue a market opportunity either party could not pursue on their own. Sometimes members of the same channel cooperate, sometimes firms in different channels partner up. Such instances are also called **cross-promotion**. In a cross-promotion situation, partners combine capital, production capabilities and other resources towards some common promotion objective beneficial to the collective. Roles are divided according to the capabilities of each firm, and proceeds are divided according to an agreed upon formula. Since both firms are dependent on each other for success, the potential for enduring conflict is lessened. However, a mechanism is needed to mediate on contentious issues.

One of the drawbacks to a horizontal marketing channel system is that it promotes short-term profit seeking behaviour. Solely focusing on the short-term will lead to the situation where marketers cross-promote dissimilar products together. When two dissimilar products are cross-promoted, the marketer must take into account the suitability of the two products. For example, Bob Dylan, the ageless rock star, counter-culture promoter and shall we say, not the handsomest of men, was once featured on the front cover of a Victoria Secret catalogue, which as many know is renowned for full page pictures of supermodels wearing the company's latest line of lingerie. Unless it's an expression of post-modern advertising, we find it difficult to understand what is the connection between the two.

HYBRID MARKETING CHANNELS

Finally, the third type of distribution system that allows a firm to dispense responsibilities and manage conflict to ensure the system functions smoothly is called a hybrid marketing channel. A hybrid marketing channel is a distribution system whereby a single firm creates more than one channel to reach one or more target markets. Also known as a multichannel distribution system, hybrid marketing channels are favoured by firms operating in large and complex markets. With multiple channels to their target markets, the firm has more opportunities to tailor the product offering to customer needs, and also expand its market coverage. These two factors enable the firm to gain more power, which translates into negotiating power to mediate in conflict and assign roles. IBM uses this approach, selling its hardware and software through its own sales force, via its stores, on the Internet and through partners such as **Value Added Resellers (VARs)** and others.

Establishing multiple channels comes with a new set of problems. As new channels develop, they will eventually compete for the same customers and sales serviced by intermediaries in the other channels. Competing against firms that are supposed to be partners will lead to conflict.

CHANNEL CONFLICT

One of the sources of conflict is change. In the business world, market conditions change all the time: new players enter, old players exit, new technologies emerge, etc. Conflict exists in every business relationship. Marketing channels are no exception.

Vertical conflict occurs when the marketing channel system employed is a vertical market channel system. This type of conflict emerges when disagreements between the manufacturer and their intermediary cannot be reconciled. Horizontal conflict occurs when firms at the same level of the channel have conflicts with each other. Franchises often complain about pricing behaviour, or other activities by other franchises operating in the same geographical region. Finally hybrid channel conflict occurs when two or more channels compete for the same market. One approach used by Unisys was to pay commission on a sale to both channels. However they found it was quite expensive and only worked for a short amount of time.

Managing the conflict requires tact, diplomacy and a sincere effort at finding common ground between the different parties. If less formal methods fail to resolve the issue, arbitration and mediation may be required to resolve long-standing disputes.

BUILDING A MARKETING CHANNEL

Every company has their own methods of reaching their target customers. Because of the wide variety, we can only provide general guidelines on how to build and manage a marketing channel.

SETTING CHANNEL GOALS AND CHANNEL TYPE

The first step is to establish the goals of the channel. The preponderant goal is to increase customer value; all other goals are secondary. Firms express their marketing objectives in terms of meeting targeted levels of customer service. Firms then decide which markets they wish to serve, and the best available types of marketing channels for reaching those segments. It is not unusual for a manufacturer to employ a vertical market channel in one market and a horizontal in another; this is particularly true in different national markets, where they may not be able to gain access to a market without a local partner.

IDENTIFYING PARTNERS

Once the company has defined the channel goals and selected the channel type, the next step is to identify partners to act as intermediaries. Choosing a partner depends on the type of distribution strategy the firm wishes to employ. One strategy, called **intensive distribution**, grants distribution rights to every possible vendor. Manufacturers of consumer goods employ this strategy, as it increases convenience for the consumer. However, because there are literally tens of thousands of partners, the marketing channel is complex and conflicts abound.

The complete opposite strategy is **exclusive distribution**. Manufacturers of luxury items often employ this strategy. Exclusive distribution grants a limited number of intermediaries exclusive rights to sell a product-line. Exclusivity increases a brand's image and desirability, and also allows for more control over pricing, promotion and customer service, since there is only one intermediary selling the product in the market. Whichever intermediary best fits the long-term goals of the manufacturer is the one that should be chosen. If you are lucky or prescient enough to gain the exclusive distribution of a hot new fashion brand in a foreign market, you may be set for life.

Finally, there is **selective distribution**. If you envision a continuum, this strategy would lie in-between intensive and exclusive distribution. With a selective distribution strategy, more than one intermediary is granted distribution rights, but not all. Deciding which firms to act as intermediaries will depend on whether the downstream players are willing to cooperate on promotional activities, adapt to meet long-term challenges and will continue to provide the lowest economic cost. Other factors to consider are profit record, sales growth, reputation, location, and size of sales force.

DESIGNING INTERNATIONAL MARKET CHANNELS

The nature of distribution channels is not uniform across borders. In fact, distribution channels are greatly affected by the cultural, economic and social development of a country. Consider North America. Usually a manufacturer makes a product, sells it to a wholesaler, who then sells it to retailers, and then to the general public. In Japan, soap passes through three wholesalers before being shelved at a retailer. Even more dramatic is the number of levels rice passes through – 23.

CHANNEL MANAGEMENT DECISIONS

Once the firm selects a partner, or a number of partners, to act as an intermediary between the manufacturer and the consumer, occasionally the leader must employ the different forms of **channel power** to elicit cooperation according to their terms.

COERCIVE POWER

The manufacturer threatens to withdraw a resource or terminate a relationship if intermediaries refuse to cooperate. In the short-term, the manufacturer will likely force the intermediary to cooperate. In the long-term however, forcing intermediaries to heel builds resentment, which could lead the intermediary to pursue strategies to negate that advantage.

REWARD POWER

Reward power is a strategy which involves offering a reward to an intermediary for cooperation. Offering incentives is more effective than coercive power, many firms use money and contests with trips and other awards as a way of enticing channels to sell their products, these are often powerful motivators.

LEGITIMATE POWER

Employing legitimate power involves requesting intermediaries to respect their contractual obligations. By making such a request, the threat of terminating the contract is implied, not stated. If the manufacturer is the dominant firm in the relationship, the intermediary will concede though no one likes it when they are leaned on and legal contracts are the centre of a conversation, the sad truth is that this is often necessary.

EXPERT POWER

Expert power is an option if the manufacturer possesses special knowledge that the intermediaries value. So long as the expertise remains with the manufacturer, the bargaining power is high. To preserve expert power, the manufacturer must continue to develop new products, processes or ideas that the intermediaries value. This is a powerful and generally well-received approach.

REFERENT POWER

Finally there is referent power. In this case, the manufacturer is so respected by consumers, the intermediaries would face financial ruin if they did not comply with the requests or demands of the manufacturer. Manufacturers like this because power remains with them and allows them to control the channel.

Power often shifts over time as the economy and the environment changes. An example of a fundamental shift of power is in the supermarket industry. In past years companies like the UK's United Biscuits, which to no one's surprise makes biscuits, would tell big supermarket chains like Tesco and Sainsbury's what biscuits customers like, because they had more data, more market research and generally more insight into the British biscuit market. However, as the supermarkets adopted more and more IT, they began to collect more and more data about consumer buying habits, including what biscuits they preferred. Over time Sainsbury's and its competitors began to tell United Biscuits what they wanted, a 180° change from the past; power had not so subtly shifted.

EVALUATING PARTNERS

Producers must evaluate the performance of their marketing channel partners. Inventory turnover, sales-quota attainment, cost of goods sold, cooperation in promotional and training programs are but some of the tests in which performance can be measured. If an intermediary is proving to be uncooperative, applying negative sanctions such as reduced margins, delayed delivery of goods, and exclusion from marketing programs should be sufficient to reform the intermediary's strategic policy. However, if a partner is cooperative but is not up to task, training and support can be offered to prop up their operations. If that proves to be unsuccessful, pruning the marketing channel is likely the best course of action, even if it is also an expensive and time consuming task to sort out new channels.

SUMMARY

- A product is a complex bundle of benefits.
- Customers relate to a product at three levels. The more levels the product appeals to, the more value the product offers.
- Product strategies such as product-line filling, and product-line stretching not only provides customers with more choice, it strengthens the company against competitive attacks.
- Marketing channels are very difficult to change once established, making them a potential source of a competitive advantage.
- Conflict is inevitable in every relationship, however, a variety of means exist to ensure cooperation.

CRITICAL QUESTIONS

1   List the core, expected and augmented product levels of a higher education. Do they differ from technical schools? How can a university change its product mix to better offer value to prospective students?
2   What are the benefits of product lining? Are there ever drawbacks? When should a product-line be pruned?
3   Why in a world of scarce resources, would a firm choose a two-way stretch?
4   What is a value network and how is it different from a supply chain?

5 Discuss the importance of intermediaries in the value network. Are there some industries where intermediaries are becoming less important?

6 Open the pages of the business section of any major newspaper. Look for stories about horizontal or vertical conflict. How would you solve the contentious issue?

SUGGESTIONS FOR FURTHER READING

Don Peppers and Martha Rogers, *Return on Customer*, New York: DoubleDay, 2005.

A new book which focuses on creating maximum value from our scarcest resource, our customer. Takes us beyond the typical measures of a business to measures that focus on the customer.

Joseph Boyett and Jimmie Boyett, *The Guru Guide to Marketing*, London, John Wiley and Sons, 2002.

A book which presents some of the best thinking of leading market gurus. A good quick way of seeing what some marketing leaders are thinking.

GLOSSARY

Augmented product level The additional services and benefits offered to a customer built around the core benefit and the expected product level.

Channel power The amount of leverage a channel member wields over their partners to elicit cooperation according to their terms.

Core benefit level The benefit or solution offered by the product the customer is buying.

Cost of capital The rate of return forgone from another investment with similar degree of risk, and maturity.

Cross-ownership A set of producers, wholesalers, and retailers who own shares in each others' companies acting in concert to maximize the returns for the collective.

Cross-promotion A set of partners who combine capital, production capabilities and other resources towards some common promotion objective beneficial to the collective.

Downstream stretch A product strategy whereby the vendor moves into a higher volume but lower profit per unit market.

Exclusive distribution   A placement strategy whereby the manufacturer grants a limited number of vendors the right to sell a product.

Expected product level   The combined features and qualities of a product that delivers its core benefit.

Intensive distribution   A placement strategy whereby the manufacturer grants distribution rights to any vendor.

Learning curve   A relationship between experience and improvements in efficiency. The more often a task is performed, the less time is required to complete the task.

Line-stretching   Lengthening the product-line to customers in up or downstream markets.

Marketing channels   An organized network of agencies and institutions which, in combination, perform all the functions required to link producers with end customers to accomplish the marketing task.

Product   A bundle of physical, psychological and experiential benefits that the customer receives that satisfies one or many wants or needs.

Product-line   The similarity between different product-lines.

Product-line depth   The number of different packaging sizes of a product.

Product-line length   The number of products sold in a product category.

Product-filling   A product strategy whereby the vendor offers the same product in different shapes, sizes, qualities or prices.

Product mix   The portfolio of products offered by a vendor.

Product-line width   The number of different product categories a vendor offers a product to.

Selective distribution   A placement strategy that grants more than one vendor the right to distribute a product, but not every vendor.

Self-cannibalization   A consequence of a product-filling strategy where the new product introduced eats into the sales or profits of other products offered by the same vendor.

Supply chain   A linear process that maps the transformations of a raw material into a finished good.

Two-way stretch   A product strategy whereby the vendor simultaneously moves into a higher margin, low volume market and a higher volume, low-margin market.

Upstream stretch A product strategy whereby the vendor moves into a higher margin but lower volume market.

Value Added Resellers (VAR) A company that modifies an existing product in order to add more value to the consumer and resells it to a customer as a new product or service.

Value network a system of interdependent organizations needed to source, support, and deliver a product that provides customers with the highest level of value.

PRICE

INTRODUCTION

After deciding which segment(s) to target, the producer must decide what price to charge their customers. Determining the right price is by no means a perfect science. First of all, different philosophies exist as to what constitutes a fair price. While there is complete agreement that the price offered must cover the cost of the product and return a profit to the producer to compensate for the risk incurred, the difficulties arise when discussing how high the realized profit should be. Athletic shoes cost pennies to make, a few dollars to advertise, and yet retail for hundreds of dollars. Selling shoes it seems is more profitable than distributing narcotics (certainly is safer). With a such a high rate of return surely, some argue, shoe manufacturers are abusing their market power and charging too high a price. That perspective ignores that consumers will pay a premium for branded and high-quality goods. As we demonstrated in the last chapter, customers like products that offer many benefits. Producers that spend resources developing their product into a brand will realize a higher profit margin, assuming the product delivers on the promises it makes to consumers. One of the great challenges for marketers in this decade is to keep prices up in spite of cheap imports from China, India and other countries. Industry after industry and country after country have seen much of their livelihood greatly affected by lower cost producers in far lands. The fashion industry is one prominent example, among many. Even the great fashion power-house of Italy, long famous for the best cloth in the world for men's suits, is seeing factory after factory closed as the quality of Chinese manufacturing continues to improve, much to China's credit. What should Italian fashion marketers do? This is a diffi-cult question but staying on the leading edge of design, cloth and manufacturing technology and thinking seems to be critical. Brands are undoubtedly part of the solution. This is a story for marketers around the world to watch.

In this chapter we outline a six-step framework on how to set the price of a product. Step 1 is to declare the marketing objective.

DECLARE THE MARKETING OBJECTIVE

The first step to determining the price of a product is to declare its **marketing objective**. The marketing objective is a stated goal a company wishes to accomplish when marketing their product at a particular price. By articulating the company's objectives, and the process in how they're going to achieve it, the possibilities of making a pricing error are reduced. There are five marketing objec-tives a company can pursue: maximize short-term profit, maximize current market share, marketing skimming or product-quality lead-ership or survival.

MAXIMIZE SHORT-TERM PROFIT

In today's business environment stock prices incur heavy losses for not meeting their expected profit targets. An unfortunate conse-quence of this reality is that most publicly traded firms employ a short-term maximizing objective. Capital almost always flows to assets where returns are perceived to be the highest. Companies that register results in excess of market expectations will be regarded as firms that create more shareholder value, which in turn maintains a high stock price. To maximize short-term profits, the firm must already understand the dynamics of their market. Having that knowledge will assist the company in making good predictions as to how their customers will react to a particular price.

Whichever price yields the highest profit, ostensibly is the price the company charges.

Maximizing current profits may allay the concerns of institutional shareholders but in emphasizing short-term profit, the company runs the risk of sacrificing long-term profits. Higher prices make substitutes more attractive. Another drawback to this strategy is that high profit levels encourage competitors to enter the market, forcing the company to split the earnings with the new entrants. What's more, demand is difficult to predict accurately. If a firm that pursues this strategy over-estimates demand, and realizes they're going to miss their profit targets, cost-cutting measures follow. The casualties of cutbacks are always research and development budgets, training programs and labour enrolment levels, which ironically are the source of future corporate revenue. Many firms in an effort to punch up this quarter's or year's results will scrimp on marketing budgets, this is most often the exact wrong thing to do if you are trying to build brand and customer loyalty.

MAXIMIZE CURRENT MARKET SHARE

To accomplish this objective, which is sometimes called market-penetration pricing, the corporation sets out to price their product such that they capture the highest amount of market share. Pricing low is an effective means of entering into a new market and building volume. The higher the volume, the lower per unit cost which eventually leads to a higher long-term profit. This objective is most successful in markets that are highly sensitive to price changes and require large-scale operations. Japanese firms had often used this approach in the past in order to gain market share in a country; they take a loss today in order to be in a much better position in a few years. Japan's more patient capital is very helpful in that it is willing to wait for these long-term results. You may also take this approach if you fear a **fast follower**, that is a competitor which will quickly jump into the market after they hear of your success. By quickly capturing market share you make it tougher for them to earn a number two position.

The drawback of a maximizing the current market share strategy is while a low price is great for consumers, short-term profit levels get hit. Unless costs are declining as volume increases, investors will tolerate stock prices for only so long. Worse still, deliberately keeping the price at a low level for extended periods of time creates a perception that the price should be always low, making it difficult to raise prices in the long-term. Such a strategy is also illegal in some markets. In markets where it takes years to start an operation (for example building an oil refinery), **dumping** a large supply of a product to reduce the market price and force other competitors to exit bears severe financial and in extreme cases, even criminal penalties.

MARKET SKIMMING

Aggressively entering a market with a low price to realize scale economies and build market share is not an appropriate strategy for products with high start-up costs and low demand much like many high-technology products. Instead manufacturers price their product in such a way that they "skim" those who are willing to pay the highest price first, and slowly reduce the price as the high payers market is exhausted. These high payers are often firms or people for whom the solution you offer is a "God send", your product fills a need which is quite important to them and could not be met, or as easily met, before. Such customers are what economists call price insensitive, that is they will pay a lot. Some pharmaceutical products are priced in this way. If the new drug will save your life or that of a loved one you tend to be less concerned about cost and more about just getting the product. Morality does not interfere with profit it seems.

High prices for cutting edge technology often create a **buzz** in the media and among the user community, and for those who can afford to purchase the item, a chance to earn social prestige. For the producer, the high price allows the firm to recoup their costs faster. Over time, the price is reduced and is marketed to the masses. Some textbooks call price skimming "riding down the demand curve". Of course, all good things must come to an end and this phase only lasts so long. The main thing that happens is that competitors rear their ugly heads. In our economic system, profit is the "blood in the water" to the sharks of capitalism; as soon as they see it they quickly are drawn to get their fair share.

PRODUCT-QUALITY LEADERSHIP

Firms that choose a product-quality strategy aim to become the innovator of the industry and offer products of the highest quality. Those that deliver on these two fronts, can use those features as part of their branding strategy, enabling them to charge a higher price than their competition. IBM takes this position often, not being on the "cutting edge" of technology but close to it, offering very innovative products with high quality. Part of IBM's offer to the market is that if you buy IBM you will get technology which is leading edge and works, unlike some of it's competitors. HP is not dissimilar, when you buy a HP laser or ink jet printer it works. Big players like these can often use FUD, or fear, uncertainty and doubt, in their sales efforts. They will make the customer wonder about buying from a smaller firm, will they be around in five years to support their product or will it be a technological orphan? Does the smaller firm have the potential to make their product a market standard? Otherwise, the customer will find it hard to hire people who know how to program for the system or run it. This is a key advantage of being a big player in an industry. The advantage of the little guy can be summarized in this one question, do you, Ms. Customer, want to be a number? Here at our small firm (OSF) you are important to us, you matter and everyone of us, up to and including the president will return your calls and make sure you get everything you need. Will IBM or HP do that for you? Of course, big or small you try to take advantage of whatever strengths your size or position offers you.

SURVIVAL

Companies pursuing survival as their strategy signals to the market that their firm is in trouble. When companies employ this strategy, the price is set just above the variable cost of production, ensuring the firm will remain operational. Operating in survival mode for long is not sustainable since competitors will employ whatever strategies to wrestle the remaining market share from their struggling rival. In the topsy-turvy airline industry we see this happening on a regular basis. In 2005 there were three main airlines in Canada, industry behemoth Air Canada, low cost carrier WestJet and third place rival Jetsgo. Jetsgo finally went bankrupt in May 2005 but not before it instigated a price war including $1 seat sales. Looking back this was a sign of great desperation as they kept creditors at the door. Ultimately it failed, though many Canadian consumers took advantage of some great prices. Within a few weeks prices for air travel in Canada soared, going up over 30% according to some analysts, and allowing Air Canada to have a great third quarter.

DETERMINE DEMAND AND SUPPLY

Once management declares the marketing objective of the product, the next step is to estimate the expected demand. Because no one can accurately predict the future correctly all the time, estimating market demand is more an art than a science. Statistical tools and methodologies greatly aid the decision making process, a seasoned manager however, knows when to go with their gut despite what the numbers may suggest. Under normal economic circumstances, relying on intuition is unnecessary because the relationship between price and quantity sold is usually inversely proportional; the higher the price, the lower the demand. Conversely, the lower the price, the higher the demand. This relationship can be illustrated by a demand curve. Before we delve into how to predict demand, we must first discuss issues related to supply.

SUPPLY SHORTAGES

The supply of a product creates exceptions to the demand-price relationship. When there's a shortage of a product, and demand is unchanged, the mechanism that balances the market is a higher price. If the supply shortage persists, a higher price increases demand, since buyers believe it is better to have the product in their hands today while supplies last. Currently there's a supply shortage in cocoa, the main ingredient used to make chocolate. Since 2003, the Ivory Coast, which produces 40% of the world's cocoa has been in a state of civil unrest. The unstable political situation has made life difficult for farmers to bring their cocoa crops to market since the plantations are on one side of the front line, the port on the other. As such, future prices for cocoa have soared. Manufacturers have been purchasing much more cocoa than they need, and storing the surplus, just in case the situation in the Ivory Coast worsens. Though chocolate prices at the retail level are unchanged, if the uncertainty persists, it is only a matter of time before manufacturers refuse to eat the price increase any more.

LUXURY GOODS

Another exception to the demand-price relationship is the existence of **luxury goods**. Luxury goods are products that are relatively price insensitive meaning demand doesn't fall as much as the price increases. As such if there's too much supply of a luxury good, consumers will reject the product causing the price to fall. The reason being is that for high involvement products, the consumer is buying the prestige associated with the product, not the product itself. This happened with Gucci in the 80s and 90s when a greedy management expanded the once exclusive brand, into many new product classes. It lost its exclusivity and cachet. Sales plummeted and only when a new CEO dramatically pruned the product mix did it regain some of its past allure.

Luxury goods also have another quirk. Demand for some luxury goods actually rises when the price rises. Economists classify these types of products as **Veblen goods**, named after economist Thorstein Veblen who believed most levels of consumption in upper classes were merely acts of displaying wealth and social status. Perfumes provide an example. For most people, especially husbands, we cannot easily tell the quality of a perfume, yet as we rush through an airport on the way home we know that it would be prudent to bring our long suffering wife a bottle of nice French perfume. What many do is use price as an indicator of quality, hence the higher the price, within limits, the more we are apt to buy that brand. Many of us may well buy wine the same way. When we have the boss and her husband over for dinner we buy an expensive wine on faith that if it is costly it must be good, real wine lovers know this is not necessarily so! Sadly for most of us, this applies for but a few product categories, for most we have to live in a world where we must reduce price to increase demand, not so good from a profitability viewpoint.

Hipster fashion icon American Apparel never goes on sale, they provide fashion basics which are timeless and seasonless. Will this be sustainable over time is an open question. Being in the retail environment they have to follow trends, for example Grouch pants were big for a few months then the moment passed, which we are all thankful for. You can make a short section run but sometime even the best retailer gets caught. If it is not sold and old you have to get rid of it.

At the heart of the issue is seeking to keep the integrity of the brand and **differentiating** the brand on the high end. But savvy and serious shoppers know they can find it somewhere, especially with the Internet, if you want to spend the time. Not everyone does.

In top end department stores, like Saks or Nordstroms or Bloomingdales, high-end fashion brands never go on sale. However, these top brand stores can negotiate with the brands, even brand powerhouses like Georgio Armani, who will give an additional 10% off if the product is not moving or they can return the merchandise. Armani then gets rid of the goods to close out stores or other discount channels.

PREDICTING DEMAND

Many models exist to predict demand. Each one measures certain variables which in turn, offer an insight on the dynamics within a market. However, due to the nature of the modelling process, some elements are always ignored. The hope is that the model ignores the inconsequential variables, or more formally stated, minimizes the error while measuring the variance between observations. As such, when estimating which of the eight states of demand your product is experiencing, it is prudent to use more than one model and subject it to many tests. We discuss three types below.

The first type of model is to use past history to predict the future. In its simplest form, the relationship between demand and price is calculated and is used to predict future behaviour. This is often used when coming up with the sales quotes for the next year, if inflation is 3% and the firm wants to grow at 5%, all quotes are raised 8% for next year. If the product is being sold in a mature market, it is plausible a simple model is all that is needed. But since markets are in a constant state of flux due to changing consumer tastes, technological innovation, and insatiable growth appetites of corporations, more complicated statistical models on which to model these forces are needed. More often than not, such elaborate models provide better results versus a simplistic model. The key to employing statistics to predict demand is to build a model that is appropriate to the market the product exists within.

A second approach is conducting price experiments. Varying the price of a product at the same store or at different locations of a franchised chain, assuming all other factors are constant, will yield an accurate portrayal of the demand curve. This can be done in supermarkets where they have many stores and it is relatively easy to do experiments like this.

Conducting market surveys is a third way to measure the demand for a product. Consumers are randomly selected and are asked questions related to how much of a product they'd buy at different price levels. Tabulating the responses will yield the demand curve. It should be noted that consumers do not make a purchase purely based on price; they evaluate how much value they are offered from the entire marketing mix. As such, surveys tend to understate a consumer's willingness to pay. An experienced manager will have a good idea by how much.

PRICE-ELASTICITY OF DEMAND

The slope of the demand curve illustrates the market's sensitivity to different prices. The more elastic the demand curve the more sensitive the market is to a price change. Visually speaking, the flatter the line the greater the effect a change in price will have on demand. Contrast this with an inelastic demand curve or steeper line, a small change in price will have a lower effect in magnitude on demand. Firms employ differentiation and branding strategies to transform their demand curve to become more inelastic. Once consumers are convinced of the differences they become less price sensitive. If branding or differentiation strategies cannot steepen the demand curve, lowering price will result in higher revenues.

ESTIMATING COSTS

Once the demand curve is estimated, the firm gains an idea of how many units they could sell given a particular price. Estimating the cost of producing the product will allow the company to properly price the product such that the rate of return will equal or exceed the expected rate of return. Of course, as much as we would like to set our prices where we can achieve our target rate of return for our corporate masters customers and competitors tend to provide a reality check for our pricing desires, they will only pay so much and only within a range of our competitors' price. Operating costs come in various forms, and we discuss a number of them in the following section.

TYPES OF COSTS

A company's cost structure takes two forms: variable and fixed. **Variable costs** depend on the level of production, while **fixed costs** are constant regardless of whether or not the company chooses to produce nothing. The sum of variable and fixed costs is called the **total cost**.

For companies that produce a handful of goods, speaking solely in terms of fixed, variable and total costs is sufficient. However, for those firms that sell millions of units, the importance of maximizing scale economies is paramount since a small increase in efficiency has a large effect in magnitude on revenue. Therefore, calculating the **average unit cost** is needed to determine the right price. Average unit cost is calculated by dividing the total cost into the level of output.

The price charged to consumers for a product must cover the total cost at a given level of production and return a profit to the firm. Otherwise the company is losing money on each item it is producing, a quick entry strategy into bankruptcy.

There are two other costs a firm must take into account when making a pricing decision, sunk costs and opportunity costs. A **sunk cost** is one that the firm already incurred and cannot recover. Trying to recoup a sunk cost is ill-advised because incorporating the additional cost of a past mistake inflates the average cost per unit. With a high average cost, the firm will require a higher rate of return on their investment. Those forgone investments are called the **opportunity cost**. When mistakes are made, it is better to write off sunk costs instead of making more investments trying to make the idea work.

ACTIVITY-BASED COST-ACCOUNTING (ABC)

Having now established some of the costs a firm must be aware of, measuring costs accurately is extremely important. One system popular with companies that conduct lots of transactions with different suppliers is called activity-based cost-accounting, or ABC. This technique identifies the relationship between an activity and the resources needed to complete it. It then assigns costs to the resources consumed by the activity. Using ABC is advantageous because it tries to account for all the resources used in a company to serve a customer: production, resource acquisition, administrative fees and others. This allows the company to accurately gauge how much of their resources are consumed serving a customer. A variation on ABC has become popular in the last few years, the **customer pyramid**. This is an important topic and one that is getting increasing attention. It is one of the best ways of improving profits. The idea is a deceptively simple one. Segment your customers based on profitability and then treat them differently. The underlying principle is one all too few companies put into action. That is, customers differ, dramatically, on their ability to deliver consistent profits to your bottom line.

Picture a pyramid with four tiers or segments. The top tier is the Platinum customers, the next Gold, the third is Iron and finally at the bottom, where they belong, Lead customers. Actually, Lead customers don't belong at all in your **customer pyramid**. This is usually the first group to action and they are an ugly lot. Lead customers, are actually nice people, one-on-one, however we must get rid of them because they cost us money every time we deal with them. This is illogical Spock. And you can't make it up on volume! What we must do is clear, upgrade them to at least Iron Customers or fire them! Sounds like we have been watching too much Donald Trump television but in this case the saying fits. The first strategy is to convert our Lead into Iron customers, that is customers which make us a profit and have potential to become the much more lucrative Gold and Platinums over time. How do you do this? A popular method is to adopt a leaner business model to do business with them. For example, instead of using your most expensive marketing tool, your sales force, use inside salespeople or e-commerce to deal with them. If this results in the same or marginally less business but with considerably reduced costs they have now been promoted to Iron customers. Another approach which we have seen used with considerable success is to have a sales manager sit down with B2B customers and tell them frankly that you are losing money dealing with them, as business people they should fully understand this problem. Discuss with them how to best deal with the issue, first can they offer you a bigger share of their spend or can you provide them less service? The formula is simple: more revenue in order to make them profitable or a less service intense business model to reduce your costs. Either way you win. If they baulk, wish them well dealing with your competitors. Be unfailingly polite and respectful of their past relationship with you and, in my experience, all will go well. We have never had nor even heard of a customer being very upset about this when done appropriately. One exception should be made when dealing with Lead customers, some Lead customers are strategically important, perhaps because of their importance as references, or because they will be the next Microsoft), or perhaps because they provide large volumes to keep your production going. In that case we let sales-people keep a small percentage, without even explanation, of lead customers.

A key problem that many firms run into implementing this approach is trying to have one employee, whether external sales, internal sales or customer service rep provide two quite different levels of service. Imagine that hotel chain Four Seasons decided in a moment of lost concentration to buy the Motel Six chain. What would it be like if you transferred a front desk clerk from the Motel Six to a Four Seasons and visa versa? The image is rather comical, both sets of customers would be quickly outraged by the normal behaviour of the front desk clerk from the other world. The Motel Six business model means that the front desk must move each new customer through in short order. Meanwhile at a Four Seasons, it is expensive, but the service, you can complain about your day to the clerk checking you as long as your heart desires! Now this perhaps is an extreme example but the principle remains. It is nearly impossible for one person to offer great service to one customer and then offer a considerably though appropriate level of service on the next call. When you have two customer service levels you almost always have to have two separate organizations.

A firm must always try to renew their top or platinum customers, as they are central to profitability, sadly, platinum customers are lost every year. They go out of business, they leave the country, our product is no longer relevant to their needs (when an executive retires they may go from the highest level of frequent flyer to almost no travel almost over night) or a competitor may win them over.

LEARNING CURVE EFFECT

The learning curve effect can be considered a contra-cost. It states that the more often a task is performed, the less cost will be incurred in the future. This relationship between experience and accumulated production has been the source of commentary for hundreds of years. But it wasn't until 1925 that it was closely studied. At the Wright-Patterson Air Force Base in the United States, engineers discovered as aircraft production doubled, the assembling time decreased by 10% to 15%, regardless of the size of the plant. Studies on other industries yielded similar results. The more workers produced an item, the more productive they became, yet the learning curve gains were the same regardless of plant size. The realized efficiency level varied between industries, but amazingly, the maxim that the learning curve effect affects an operation regardless of scale remains largely true.

Being the first manufacturer to maximize the learning curve gives the firm a substantial advantage over its competitors. Because per unit costs are lower, it can use that cost advantage for one of three things – to give a lower price to customers making it harder for competitors to compete profitably. Secondly, spend that extra money on brand building and other marketing activities to differentiate your product from competitors or thirdly, just be more profitable. Once the competition has caught up, the firm should reassess the strategic importance of the business.

ANALYSING COMPETITORS' COSTS, PRICES AND OFFERS TO POSITION THE PRODUCT

By this stage, the price of the product is beginning to take shape: the demand curve provides an insight as to the market's responsiveness to different prices, and the optimal cost structure is determined. At this stage, the product should be evaluated against the competition using a balanced scorecard. By comparing the competitor's product offering, which includes price and features, the appropriate price range is clear, enabling the firm to move to step five, which is selecting the appropriate price method.

SELECTING A PRICE METHOD

There are a wide range of pricing methods available to the firm, each with their own advantages and disadvantages. We discuss a number of them.

MARKUP PRICING

A markup pricing scheme entails adding a markup over the cost of producing one unit. This pricing method is widely used by manufacturers of mass-merchandise and professionals working in service industries. Below is an example of how markup pricing works.

Let us suppose a mid-career manager inherits a million dollars from a beloved aunt who happened to be a shrewd investor. The inheritance is enough start-up capital to buy all the necessary equipment to open up a high-scale restaurant, the mid-career manager's dream job.

Because our restaurateur has some managerial expertise, she knows going into the business is risky, and believes a rate of return of 30% will adequately compensate her for her troubles. Her cost structure is as follows:

Variable Cost (inc. labour)	$5
Fixed Costs	$1,000,000
Expected Sales	80,000

Before calculating the markup, our entrepreneur must know the cost per unit. The formula is as follows:

Unit cost = Variable Cost + (Fixed Costs/Unit Sales)

Plugging our numbers into the formula yields:

Unit Cost = $5 + ($1,000,000/80,000)
Unit Cost = $17.50

Each plate costs her $17.50. To calculate the markup price, the formula is:

$$\text{Markup Price} = \text{unit cost}/(1 - \text{expected rate of return})$$
$$= \$17.5/(1 - 0.30)$$
$$= \$25$$

She would have to charge $25 per plate to achieve a 30% rate of return.

Markup pricing is often referred to as fair pricing. It allows the producer to cover their costs and earn a fair rate of return. However, markup pricing ignores the consumer's perceived-value of the product. As we demonstrated in the last chapter, products that offer many benefits command a higher price in the marketplace. Fair pricing also ignores the hard reality of competitor's pricing which in effect provides a ceiling which we cannot rise above unless we have successfully differentiated our product in a way relevant to the customer so that they are willing to pay a premium.

TARGET RETURN PRICING

Target Return pricing involves setting a price that yields an expected return on investment. Do not confuse return on investment (ROI) with the expected rate of return. The former calculates the effectiveness of the capital spent, the latter, is the opportunity cost. The formula for ROI is expressed as follows.

$$\text{Target Return Price (TRP)} = \text{unit cost} + \frac{[(\text{opportunity cost}) \times (\text{fixed costs})]}{\text{unit sales}}$$

Returning to our example above, the target return price for our restaurateur would be:

$$\text{TRP} = \$17.50 + \frac{(30\% \times 1,000,000)}{80,000}$$

She will earn a 30% ROI if their product is priced at $21.25.

One advantage of using the TRP scheme is that it allows the company to estimate their **break-even point** should sales not reach the expected amount. As the name suggests, the break-even point is the least amount of units needed to be sold in order for the firm to recover their production costs. Recall, the total cost is the sum of the variable cost and the fixed cost. Where the total cost curve intersects with the projected revenue curve is the firm's break-even point. Mathematically, it can be expressed as:

Break-even volume = Fixed Costs/(Price – variable cost)

Plugging in the numbers from our culinary example yields:

$$\text{Break-even volume} = 1{,}000{,}000/(\$25 - \$5)$$
$$= 50{,}000 \text{ units.}$$

Our restaurateur must sell 50,000 plates of food to cover her operating expenses.

PERCEIVED-VALUE PRICING

The drawback to the previous two pricing methods is that they aggregate consumers into one group. In reality there are different types of consumers, each has a different perception as to what the price of the product should be. Some purchase a good because of the price, some buy a good because of the quality and features, while others buy products because they are concerned about price and do not take into account the power of the brand. Brands reduce uncertainty, and the consumer is willing to pay a premium to eliminate it. Discovering exactly how high that premium is depends on the value the consumer places on the product's features and other marketing-mix elements. That value will always be changing and requires constant monitoring. This is even more important on the Business-to-Business (B2B) side of marketing. Value based marketing and pricing is critical for many firms.

In many industries there are two basic business models. In the high-tech industry for example, there is generally a low cost or **black box** model which focuses almost solely on price and that is their prime selling proposition. We call it black box because they do not discuss or often even know what the technology is inside the box. In contrast is the full service vendor who not only has the box but also understands the technology inside it: they offer great service, advice on how to use the technology in your business and thus adds very considerable value to the basic hardware itself. The problem is that you must effectively communicate the extra value that your business model creates for the customer in a way that they will be willing to pay the higher price necessitated by your full service model. This is not easy with a black box competitor lingering around because they will keep hammering home their one simple point – they are cheaper! This is what they call a "no brainer" decision, we are just as good but 25 % cheaper. But many firms, including IBM manage to effectively communicate their value and win their fair share of business.

VALUE PRICING

Value pricing is a method where the producer charges a low price for a higher-quality good. Large retailers often employ this pricing method to attract customers to their stores. Once within the store, the customer is more inclined to purchase non-advertised goods because of the convenience of buying all of their goods under one roof. To some degree Wal-Mart has a value pricing model with lower prices on reasonable quality goods; due to their incredible volumes they can negotiate the best price from virtually every manufacturer they deal with. One friend of ours sold to Wal-Mart and his firm had to agree that Wal-Mart would get the best price in the country which makes it easier for Wal-Mart to under price their competitors and still be quite profitable. This idea also leads to the phenomenon of **loss leaders,** that is that some retailers, supermarkets for example, realize that very few customers know the prices for more than a few goods in their shop. Think of what prices you know of goods you regularly buy at a supermarket, we can only think of milk and beer! What these stores do is make sure they have low prices on those few items, that consumers know so when customers see those low prices they assume that other prices are also low, creating a positive halo effect of low cost for the store.

GOING-RATE PRICING

Going-rate pricing entails the producer pricing their product strictly according to the price charged by competition. This pricing method is often found in commodities markets, where the differentiation between products is virtually nil. Marketers hate commodities because it is hard to make a profit unless you are the lowest cost producer; of course, there is logically only one low cost producer so every other firm competing with them will be scrambling for profit. That is why marketers always try to differentiate in a way relevant to the customer and in a way that the customer will accept that you really are different from your competition. It doesn't always work but nevertheless we never give up the good fight! One time one of us taught the Vice President of Marketing for the Canadian Wheat Board. Talk about a potentially undifferentiated product – the government of Canada certifies that the wheat is Grade A and so on. Yet he said that they manage to differentiate what is almost the same physical product in 24 different ways. For example they sell the wheat to Italy for pasta and alter the product to make it better for pasta making, something evidently quite important in Italy. Meat firm, Maple Leaf Foods works with farmers to raise pigs which have been bred specifically for the demanding Japanese market, allowing them to charge a healthy premium for a product for which Japanese consumers are happy to pay extra so everybody wins.

AUCTION PRICING

The attraction of the auction is that it saves the producer the trouble in determining the consumer's perceived value of the product; the auction allows the consumer to do so on their own accord. There are three types of auctions:

DUTCH AUCTION

When Google became a publicly traded company, they chose the unusual approach of selecting a Dutch auction method to sell their shares. In this system, the bidding starts with the highest price, reflecting the maximum value the seller believes the product is worth. Then price slowly decreases until the bidder agrees to the price. The price continues to decrease until the entire stock is sold.

ENGLISH AUCTION

An English-style auction is the opposite of a Dutch auction. A minimum price is set, and bidders continue to raise their offers, until the person who wants the good the most outbids the competition. This is the most popular of bidding systems.

SEALED BIDS

A sealed bid system is often employed by a buyer who wants to extract the lowest price from a group of sellers who offer relatively similar goods or services. In a sealed bid system, the bidders are prevented from knowing the value of other proposed bids. That lack of information forces the seller – in theory at least – not to bid below their cost, and not to bid too high otherwise they'll lose the contract. Whenever the government announces a public works program, they invite bidders to participate in a sealed bid auction. Transparency and having lots of bidders are two requirements to ensure the process is competitive. This is widely used by government and when ignored a political scandal often ensues, as has happened in Germany, England and the US in recent years. Even if the governing party doesn't tamper with the bidding process, there is a potential for bidders to get together and agree to rig the price; this is called collusion and is illegal.

GROUP PRICING

Finally, group pricing is a method where a group of buyers pool their resources, and use their buying power to negotiate a lower price from the seller. Vendors are more likely to reduce the per-unit cost if they sell larger quantities. Therefore group pricing is an attractive option for buyers with the same interests. This is used by buying groups in retail who try to at least partially play catch up with Wal-Mart by buying together in quantities closer to Wal-Mart's enormous volumes. This was also quite big during the dotcom boom when buying groups used the Internet to help in the process and though the dotcom boom has gone bust there are still groups successfully doing this.

SELECTING THE PRICE

Before settling on the final price, there are other elements that must be discussed that aid the company in selecting a price. They are psychological pricing, gain and risk sharing.

PSYCHOLOGICAL PRICING

Information plays a primary role in a consumer's mind as they formulate their perceived value of a product. Elements such as price of substitutes, advertising, consumer-advocacy reports and the reputation of the company contribute to brand equity. Eventually, the consumer decides what the price of a product should be, any deviation from that price is either a bargain, or too expensive. Marketers call this perceived price a **reference price**. Research has shown that consumers are more willing to buy a product if the retail price is listed as $999 than if it were priced at $1,000. The psychological barrier between 999 and 1000 is larger than the difference of a dollar.

GAIN AND RISK SHARING PRICING

A GRS pricing method is a guarantee on the part of the supplier to deliver on the promises about the product. Should the product not meet the consumer's satisfaction, the customer can return the product and obtain a refund. Reducing the risk the consumer is exposed to makes the decision to buy a product more favourable.

PRICE DISCRIMINATION

As the name suggests, price discrimination is a method of charging different prices for the same product to different consumers. For this system to work, the producer must be able to segment the market. Second, trading between different segments is impossible. Third, competitors cannot directly compete against the producer. Fourth, consumers accept that price discrimination does occur. Fifth, the cost of segmenting and enforcing the method is less than the revenue generated. And finally, it must be legal.

Price discrimination occurs in many industries. Software companies for example charge corporations a much higher fee than individual users. Airlines steadily increase the cost of flying as the departure date nears. Many nightclubs charge different entrance fees for males and females. If conducted correctly, price discrimination will result in higher revenue for the company. What we see in a number of industries is that price discrimination is becoming harder to pull off today. Widespread use of the Internet means that people are less apt to accept price discrimination. Airlines for example are beginning to move to simpler and more transparent airfare structures because of customer upset over the fact that the person beside them on the plane paid a much lower fare. The old need to stay over a Saturday night or an American on a visit to Europe having to stay for a minimum of seven days is no longer required by many airlines, it is simply not sustainable any more. We always wondered why European authorities would insist that North Americans must at minimum go to Europe for 7 days; were we that desperate in need for long exposure to European culture? What is much more widely known now was that it was not a government requirement but a way for airlines to get frequent travellers to pay a high premium for the privilege of going over to London or Paris for just a day or two.

GEOGRAPHICAL PRICING

Geographical pricing is employed when a company sells the same product in different locations. Because the product must be delivered to different places, the logistical cost is directly proportional to the distance. As such, the producer must charge a higher price for goods that are furthest from the plant. However, the price the producer charges their most distant markets is tempered by the price of substitutes in the local market and the potential for arbitrage, where a third party decides to buy the product in the cheap market and resell it in the more expensive one. In some cases trading does occur, we call this **grey marketing**, which refers to the flow of goods through distribution channels other than those authorized by the manufacturer or producer. This, unlike black markets, is not illegal but often intensely disliked by the manufacturer because it reduces profitability. Frequently this occurs when the price of an item is significantly higher in one country than another. Electronic goods and pharmaceuticals are two common products where this occurs. Entrepreneurs will buy the product where it is available cheaply, import it legally to the target market and sell it a price which provides a healthy profit but which is below the normal market price there. This is a particular problem when the price is higher in another country not because of price gouging but simply because it is more expensive to do business in the one country. For example, London is expensive, retail rentals, office space, eating out and simply just living. It is only fair that firms who sell there charge more than lower cost Greece. It does cost Nikon profit though when a Briton on holiday in Greece picks up a Nikon camera there at a lower price and brings it back to London and expects Nikon to honour the warranty in his home country.

OTHER MARKETING-MIX ELEMENTS

Because markets are not perfectly competitive, information plays a vital role in the decision making process. As such, consumers will pay a premium for products that are of good quality and well-advertised instead of buying products of comparable quality that are not as well-known. In the world of high-tech there is a saying that "You don't get fired for buying IBM". What this saying means is that IBM is widely accepted as having top quality, if it breaks down, that is just the vicissitudes of life, not because you bought cheap and saved money at the moment of purchase but paid through the nose later on when the system broke down. That is also why many people will a premium for a well-known brand. We will pay more for a Ralph Lauren shirt not just for the pony on the chest to impress my friends with my social cachet but also because it is a symbol of quality, to put it in the words of a recent advertising slogan, "Mr. Lauren don't make no bad things". What's more, providing customer-service for after sales assistance, reliable delivery schedules and a commitment to preserve the quality of the product are important factors in the decision making process. Reducing the **cognitive dissonance** of the consumer leads to a higher likelihood they will select the product, even if it means paying a premium.

SUMMARY

- Price is most flexible of the marketing Ps.
- The perceived value of goods varies between individuals.
- Setting the price is a six-step process that starts with defining the marketing objective and ends with the price selected.
- The required rate of return is a primary factor in establishing the minimum price charged.
- Customers always have a reference price in mind when making a purchasing decision.

CRITICAL QUESTIONS

1   Compare and contrast the various marketing objectives a firm can pursue. If you were the manager of a leading company and you were faced with the prospect of fighting off a big competitor, which would you choose? What if the competitor was a small start-up?
2   Discuss how price can be adjusted to take into account the different types of customers that exist.
3   Identify the internal factors that influence the price charged.
4   What are the unique features of luxury goods with respect to market demand?

SUGGESTIONS FOR FURTHER READING

James Anderson and James Narus, *Business Market Management: Understanding, Creating and Delivering Value*, New York, Prentice Hall, 1998.

In more and more markets the idea of value based marketing is taking great importance. How do you get away from being a commodity and show the value of your business model to your customers? This an excellent book to give you a sound in-depth perspective on this important topic.

Neil Rackham and John DeVincentis, *Rethinking the Sales Force: Redefining Selling to Create and Capture Customer Value*, New York, McGraw-Hill, 1999.

Our sales force is one of most powerful tools. These two authors have contributed a lot to our thinking on today's sales approach. This book helps think about how our sales force can sell the idea of value to our customers.

GLOSSARY

Activity based cost accounting   A system of assigning costs directly to the resources used in the production process.

Auction pricing   A pricing method where the customer sets their own price according to his or her perceived value of the product.

Average unit cost   The quotient from dividing the total cost into the level of output.

Break-even point   The minimum number of units that need to be sold to ensure the firm recovers their operating expenses.

Black box   A term used to describe the process a buyer undergoes when making a purchasing decision.

Cognitive dissonance   The discomfort felt by a person when faced with choices that contradict the individual's personal values, beliefs or attitudes. This conflict drives the individual to select the option that minimizes the tension.

Customer pyramid   A model that proposes marketers segment their customers into classes, from the most profitable to the least, and only target their resources towards those that do or can purchase more products or services.

Differentiating   A strategy a seller uses to distance their product from another by emphasizing its unique features, benefits or qualities.

Dumping   When a company charges either less than it costs or less than it charges in its home market, in order to buy their way into a market or capture high market share.

Fast follower   A nimble competitor who can enter profitable markets quickly.

Fixed costs   Expenses incurred by the business that remain constant despite the level of production.

Loss leaders   Deliberately selling a product below cost to attract customers.

Luxury goods   A good where rising prices results in a less than proportional drop in demand.

Geographical pricing　A pricing method whereby the price charged differs in different geographic locations.

Going-rate pricing　A pricing method used for commodities where the price charged is the same charged by the competition.

Grey marketing　Products sold through marketing channels not approved by the manufacturer.

Group pricing　A pricing method whereby a group of buyers agree to share resources to increase their bargaining power with a much larger sized supplier.

Marketing objective　A stated goal a company wishes to accomplish by selecting a particular price for their product.

Market skimming　Setting the price of a product at the highest possible level, and over time gradually reducing the price to attract new but less needy customers.

Markup pricing　A method of pricing whereby the producer adds a premium to the cost of the product to ensure the profit earned will equal at least the opportunity cost of the investment.

Opportunity cost　The forgone return from making one investment over another with similar risk profiles.

Perceived-value pricing　Pricing goods according to how customers perceive the value they receive from consuming a product.

Price discrimination　A pricing method whereby a different price is charged according to a customer's willingness to pay.

Psychological pricing　A pricing method that lessens the cognitive dissonance of making a purchasing decision.

Reference price　The price consumers believe a product should be sold at.

Sunk cost　An irrecoverable expense.

Target return pricing　A method of pricing that ensures the total profit will equal the expected return on investment.

Total cost　The sum of all variable and fixed costs.

Variable costs　Expenses incurred by the business that change in proportion to the amount of product produced.

Veblen goods　A good where rising prices results in higher demand.

5

PROMOTION

PROMOTION

Promotion is the fourth element of the marketing mix. Being successful in this element of the marketing mix not only builds good publicity for the firm itself, but the brand equity of its products also prospers. Promotion involves disseminating information about a product or a company using five different key types of promotions: advertising, sales promotion, public relations, personal selling and direct marketing. Together, the five elements are all part of a company's **promotion mix**. Each type of promotion employs a different set of approaches to communicate with the current and prospective customer. Since each type of promotional tool interacts with customers differently, the whole promotional mix must be integrated to deliver a consistent message regarding the strategic positioning of the company, and information regarding the product and the value it offers.

THE COMMUNICATION PROCESS

Regardless of the type of communication involved, there is a communicator, an audience, a channel and a message. The communicator is the person or company sending the message to the audience, who are either potential or current customers. The channel is the medium which the message travels through and finally the message itself, which is the information the marketer wishes to disseminate. Though this is simple to say, even the best-designed message faces difficulties reaching the intended audience. Once the message is released through one or many channels, it must permeate through the tens of thousands of other messages sent by other marketers who are trying to attract the attention of the audience. If the message manages to diffuse through the clutter and reach the audience, it faces another hurdle: studies estimate the average American adult receives in excess of 3,000 messages everyday. This is not to say that the average American is simply sitting around watching television all day! When a bus goes by, it has multiple messages on the side. A co-worker walks into a meeting with a Starbucks coffee cup and a Nike sweater on, two more exposures. You watch ER and the plot includes a Lincoln car, another exposure this time to a product placement in a leading show. It is impossible for a person to absorb and respond to that much information. Rather than be over stimulated and go nuts, most consumers in the developed world simply have learned to ignore most messages. This is a huge challenge for marketers.

There are more issues. Over the last two decades significant changes have occurred in the media industry. Due mostly to technological innovation, the number of channels to reach potential and current customers has exploded. But while the total number of channels has increased, the size of the audience remains relatively stable. In other words, mass media channels have been fragmented into smaller, more focused channels catering to special-interest audiences. Today there is much more than TV; there are hundreds of satellite radio stations, podcasts, and the biggest change of all, the ubiquitous Internet. For marketers **media fragmentation** is both a boon and a curse; it translates into an opportunity to craft better messages for a particular audience. The opportunity to customize the promotional mix to small groups introduces the risk of sending conflicting messages to different audiences. **Podcasts** are an intriguing example. Podcasts are free audio broadcasts, available through websites or directories such as iTunes that can be downloaded to your MP3 player or your computer. You can subscribe to programs from large, well-known networks such as

CNN, ABC (Australian Broadcasting Company) and BBC or download obscure offerings produced as a hobby by people in their basements. It is difficult to come up with an accurate figure for the number of podcasts available. iTunes offers 20,000 podcasts alone and that number is growing by 1,000 a week, according to Steve Jobs, chief executive officer of Apple Computer. Another popular directory, Podcastalley, has more than 13,150 podcasts available and another 158 pending approval. By the time you read this book these figures will be sadly out of date. Some firms are starting their podcasts or blogs in order to reach out directly to their potential customers. As marketers, this is an area where we are still mucking about figuring out how we take advantage of these new media to effectively reach our target markets. One of the first and primary lessons is about authenticity. Customers expect to hear the real and honest voice of the firm. Spinning an issue is not on in podcasts and blogs – listeners and readers want truth.

To ensure a consistent message about the company and its products is being sent, many firms are now adopting an **integrated marketing communications (IMC)** approach. Using this approach, the firm coordinates all promotion activities to ensure the same message about the company and its products are delivered to all points of contact the customer encounters. This can be a complex business for a large consumer goods firm like Procter & Gamble, Unilever or Kao; television, radio, newspapers, magazines, salespeople, distributors, and now blogs, podcasts and product placements in movies and television shows, all singing from the same hymn sheet – a tough thing to pull off. But pull it off we must try.

DEVELOPING AN INTEGRATED MARKETING COMMUNICATIONS STRATEGY
IDENTIFY THE TARGET AUDIENCE

The first step is to identify the target audience. The audience can be the general public, a special interest group, or even an individual. Choosing the target audience and the response sought are crucial because the content of the message, the manner in which it is relayed and the channels it travels through are all dependent at whom the message is targeted.

CHOOSE THE DESIRED RESPONSE

The marketer can choose between *informing* the audience about a new product, *repositioning* a product or the company itself, or *reinforcing* a brand or company's image. However, in most cases, *persuading* the audience to make a purchase is the desired response. Consumers rarely make impulse purchases, especially on expensive items which we earlier called high involvement goods; they gather facts before they're ready to buy. A model called the **hierarchy of effects model** traces the six stages consumers typically pass through before making a purchase. The desired response sought is to move the audience from one stage to another. Early in a marketing campaign the results measure of the success of your market efforts is if you have moved potential customers from one stage to the next; of course, the ultimate goal is to turn them into customers and loyal ones at that, but it is a process you build a stage at a time.

The first is the *awareness* stage. Consumers residing in this stage have either never heard of the firm or are uncertain of the benefits offered by the firm's products. The objective in this case would be to design a promotion mix that increases the consumer awareness around the product or the firm itself. Danone, a French based multinational that produces a wide variety of yogurt products, is facing considerable difficulties convincing North American consumers that fortified yogurt is more than just a dairy product, it is also a suitable and healthy snack food. Much of their current marketing strategy in North America involves handing out free samples supplemented by an advertising campaign that repeatedly connects their product to healthy and active lifestyles.

The second stage is *knowledge*. Consumers in this stage of the buying process recognize the product, but do not possess enough information to make an informed decision. Marketers must determine which information the target audience lacks and design a message that fills the gap.

Once the audience is aware of a product and understands the benefits offered; the marketer tries to move their target audience through the final stages of the buying process by making consumers feel better about making the purchase. The third stage is *liking*, which entails creating positive messages to promote the product. This is where the emotional part of the marketing kicks in. In some cases, especially with low involvement goods, consumers may largely skip the knowledge stage and go straight to liking. Many Coke ads are simply getting us to feel a warm positive glow about Coke so when we pitch up at the supermarket we feel subconsciously drawn toward Coke, because we a have a positive emotional response to it. *Preference* is the fourth stage. Think of Coke ads at Christmas time which generally consist of attractive people singing beautiful music about living together in harmony, an admirable sentiment but we are not sure what that has to do with product advantages of Coke over arch-rival Pepsi.

At this point, the marketer explains to consumers why their product should be at the top of their list. If consumers agree with the self-assessment, they move to the fifth stage, *conviction*. Finally, other promotional offers such as rebates, free upgrades or similar tools can be employed to nudge the reluctant buyer to make a purchase. You often will see this on ads on television selling music or books where they will throw in another product free if you buy now, now, now! In marketing parlance this is a call for action in the moment. If you buy today you will also receive a free ginsu knife set. Marketers realize that for many if you do not take action in store you will probably not come back. That is why salespeople in an electronics or white goods (e.g. kitchen appliance) store work so hard to get you to buy right now, if you don't, they view you as a lost sale as you walk out the door. Of course, you may well honestly only want to see what they have on offer at the competitor's store down the road and may well come back in a few minutes, however experienced salespeople are mainly right, you will generally not return.

DESIGN THE MESSAGE

The next step is to design a message that garnishes the desired response. For a message to be effective, it must grab the audience's attention, hold their interest long enough to listen to the offering, then stimulate a desire to take action – this sequence is known as AIDA.

MESSAGE CONTENT

The success of implementing the AIDA model depends on the content of the message. Research has shown there are three forms that are proven to solicit a response: rational, moral and emotional messages. Rational messages typically entail comparing the advertised product to another through a demonstration of how the product offers increased economy, higher performance, or higher quality or some other feature relevant to the target market.

Messages with a moral are crafted to appeal to the audience's sense of right and wrong. Appeals to the audience moral code is usually practised by organizations promoting such public services as safe driving, trying to encourage you to practice safe sex, stop smoking, send money to help those in a disaster area, etc.

Finally, emotional messages attempt to stir an emotional response to move consumers from one stage in the buying process to another. Often emotional messages are designed to scare, guilt or shame the recipient into action. The use of airbrushed supermodels for example is known to contribute to such mental illnesses as anorexia nervosa because images of an unobtainable ideal degrades already low levels of confidence in adolescent teenage girls.

However, not all emotional messages are negative minded. Those that appeal to one's sense of humour, pride or irony are positive messages. Unfortunately there is still lingering doubt that positive messages, particularly those that rely on humour actually translates into sales. Critics contend using humour only entertains and merely distracts the audience from the true purpose of the message, which is to buy. A rather dour perspective.

We live in an age where consumers make purchasing choices between very similar products. More often than not, the product selected was not the one that was heavily advertised, but rather the one that garnished the highest level of brand equity. Shoppers are not as logical as we think. Creating messages that promote a positive image positively affects brand equity. The recipient might not run to the store immediately once they watch a humorous advertisement. But who can forget a good laugh?

MESSAGE SOURCE

A second factor in determining the success of a message relates to the likeability and trustworthiness of the source itself. Research has shown the audience is more likely to identify with or aspire to the recommendations of an attractive source versus one that is considered unattractive. Using celebrity spokespeople has long been a favoured approach by advertisers to promote their product. Love them or hate them, endorsements from celebrities such as Celine Dion and David Beckham can turn even the most staid product into a hot commodity. Oprah Winfrey's book club is an example of the power of a source. A positive review from Oprah can lead to extraordinary sales and authors long for her approval. According to a recent article in *Chicago Tribune*, "Jim Milliot, business and news director at industry magazine *Publishers Weekly*, said that a 'respectable' new fiction release should sell about 40,000 books annually. If Oprah chooses a book, sales will easily jump well into the six figures and sometimes past 1 million". Of course there is a downside which firms which use supermodel Kate Moss or singer Michael Jackson have learned, if their spokesperson has a problem it may well cast a negative light on their product as well and you had better ditch that superstar superquick.

One would think that the source's credibility plays a significant role. Interestingly, so long as the message remains one-sided, the credibility of the source isn't a factor in the long-term. This "sleeper effect" phenomenon was discovered by psychologist Carl Hoyland shortly after the World War II. He wanted to study the effects of war propaganda films on American soldiers. To his surprise, even though soldiers disbelieved the authenticity of Soviet propaganda films, over time their attitudes changed some-what. Strangely, while they could recall the content of the message, they could not identify the source. Familiarity does indeed breed liking.

MESSAGE FORMAT

The format of medium that the message travels through is also an important factor to consider. Using print media requires the marketer to craft headlines, illustrations and use combinations of colours that are appealing to the target audience. Whereas in radio broadcasting, the voice of the announcer, the types of words used and sound modulations are all arranged to create images in the mind of the target audience. Television broadcasting overcomes the problem of creating pictures; they simply display them. But a good picture alone doesn't tell the whole story. Subtle cues such as facial expressions, gestures, and posture contribute to the overall effectiveness of a message. Finally, even the package itself communicates a message. The size, shape, colour, scent, texture and font communicate to the audience the value the product contains. Each medium has its own quirks and special things you need to know. For example at movie theatres you typically have ads displayed before the movie begins. The nice thing is that you have a captive audience which is probably going to pay attention; on the other hand you don't want to just show them ads they would see at home. You should really take advantage of the big screen plus you *must* remember they paid to be in those seats, unlike at home where, whether they realize it or not they are watching free television because of the commercials, so you have to adjust your content to suit that reality.

Having discussed the theory of communication and various strategies to ensure the chances a message reaches the intended receiver, we now examine the various tools of the promotion mix.

SELECT THE COMMUNICATION CHANNELS

Now that a message has been constructed, and the source to transmit the message is identified, the manager must select between personal and non-personal communication channels to reach their target audiences. Personal communication channels involve two or more people communicating directly to each other. This includes using a telephone, email or regular mail, satellite television, or simply face to face. Whereas non-personal communication channels involve using the media to transmit the message. More on the advantages of each later.

ESTABLISHING THE BUDGET

Traditionally, there is a tension between marketing managers and financial managers. Marketers believed that the product that was the most heavily promoted would be the product that succeeds in the market. Financial managers, who agree with that assessment for the most part, temper the enthusiasm with the droll reality that resources are not unlimited; a corporation exists to maximize profit. Because of this tension, compromises must be reached in establishing the communications budget.

AFFORDABLE METHOD AND COMPETITIVE PARITY METHOD

The affordable method is an ad-hoc approach to establishing a communications budget. Often it entails a manager asking the accounting department what is the most that can be spent on advertising. This approach can work if high demand exists for the product, or if the company is a small firm, where formalities are blurred. However, if this method is employed in a medium to large sized organization it leads to chaos. Without a reliable budget, marketers cannot forge long-term promotion plans, and financial managers cannot reliably forecast future profits.

The competitive parity method is also an ad-hoc approach to establishing a communications budget. Instead of using their own expertise, the firm decides to use the expertise of their competitor to determine how much money should be spent. In other words, their communication expenditures mirror their competition's. It is not a good sign if a firm relies on the marketing expertise of their competitors, though if Coke sees Pepsi is running a big new campaign, they may well feel obliged to respond in kind.

PERCENTAGE OF SALES METHOD

A more reliable method of establishing a communications budget is to fix the budget to the performance of the product itself. In other words, though the communications budget differs according to stage of the business cycle, the percentage spent remains equal. What's more, if every competitor adopts this practice, the industry begins to demonstrate conditions that economists term market equilibrium.

As promising as the percentage of sales method sounds, there are a number of disadvantages. First, the method assumes product sales are closely correlated with the business cycle. Some products are always in demand, and that advantage can be used to gain more market share when the competition is languishing. But if the firm employed a percentage of sales method, it cannot take advantage of market opportunities. More concerning, it assumes markets are in a state of equilibrium. Markets are never in a state of equilibrium. There is a constant churning of firms entering and exiting markets, new technologies destroy old industrial structures, and managerial practices re-engineer how business is conducted. Maintaining a constant communications budget with so much turbulence, while courageous is ultimately folly, because the firm is ignoring that markets are in a constant state of flux.

OBJECTIVE AND TASK METHOD

A must superior method is the objective and task method which requires the marketer to define an objective, determine the tasks required to achieve the objective and estimate the total cost. Why it is not as widely used as we would like is because it is hard work. This method allows firms to capitalize on market opportunities as they arise. Firms choose between a **push strategy** and a **pull strategy**. A push strategy entails using different promotional tools to push the product through the channels to market. The manufacturer directs their promotional activities to convince their intermediaries to carry a product. This may include for special bonuses for the store and the salesperson to sell a particular brand or product. If several competitors do this it can lead to a bonus war which is gratifying for the salespeople but lousy for the profits of the manufacturers. The intermediaries in turn, direct their promotional activities toward the final customer. Whereas employing a pull strategy entails taking the opposite approach. The producer directs their promotional activities to the final customer, who in turn seeks the product from channel members and promotes their processors to the final consumer. Channel members in turn, react by placing more orders with the producer. Many companies use both strategies and when they work together they are the most powerful, that is a customer walks in asking for the product and the company not only has it but is enthusiastic about selling it, rather than trying to sell the person another product where they make a bigger commission. In all of their promotional material aimed at the final consumer, computer-chip maker Intel demonstrates the many benefits of using the latest microchip. Intel also insists any machine that uses an Intel chip must have a sticker on the computer that indicates one of their chips powers the machine.

Buyers also employ the same strategies to accomplish an objective. When a customer wants a new product developed, they can inform the manufacturer to build it (usually in the form of user-feedback) and then the product gets pulled through marketing channels. Or the customer could push the idea through the inter-mediary first before getting to the manufacturer. It all depends on how you look at the situation.

Marketers can elect to use a pull or push strategy to promote their product. The strategy employed depends heavily on the rela-tionship the seller has with its customers. If their product is branded as one that offers experiential benefits, a push strategy not only creates a buzz in the marketplace, but also creates a situation where the customer is requesting products to be offered, which as we mentioned earlier in the book is the ultimate aim of marketing – get the customer to come to you. So that's the aim, how do you do it? In the next section we discuss the various promotional tools at a manager's disposal.

PROMOTION TOOLS
ADVERTISING

According to the American Marketing Associate, advertising is the placement of announcements and persuasive messages in time or space purchased in any of the mass media by business firms, non-profit organizations, government agencies, and individuals who seek to inform and/or persuade members of a particular target market or audience about their products, services, organizations, or ideas. Advertising is by far the most popular means of reaching a target audience because it is a cost-effective way to build awareness in the minds of an audience. And through repeated exposure, the audience accepts the product's positioning and comes to trust the product to deliver the promised benefits.

Good advertising provides reasons to customers to buy a product or service. To create a good ad, the marketer must create a message that is distinct, meaningful and credible. Failure to do so results in the message being lost in the noise surrounding the audience. However, crafting a distinct message is but one part of an effective ad. The message must also be crafted with their interests in mind. If the message cannot demonstrate how or what extra value they receive, the audience will not react. Finally, if the audience does not believe the product, service, organization or idea delivers on the promised benefits, they dismiss the message outright.

TYPES OF MESSAGES

Slice of life   Demonstrates the product being used in a typical setting.

Statement   Challenges the audience into acting on their complacency. Benetton ads often feature graphic images of social causes such as AIDS.

Lifestyle   Demonstrates how the product is part of a lifestyle.

Fantasy   A dream or myth is created to promote a product. Some products claim they are made with "goodness inside", or were created in "hidden gardens".

Mood/image   A mood or image is crafted to surround the product. Athletic shoe manufacturers try to convince users buying the advertised shoe will improve athletic performance.

Musical   This message is conveyed through a catchy jingle or song. Billed as a tribute to a friend who died from gunshot wounds, rap star Puff Daddy remixed his friend's voice and a dance beat into a popular song released by The Police 10 years earlier. Puff Daddy was later awarded a Grammy for Best Original Song.

Technical Expertise   This type of message demonstrates the company's expertise in making a product or service they offer.

Spokesperson   This message features a figure in popular culture or a recognized authority endorsing the product. So long as the target audience trusts the spokesperson, the endorsement is credible.

Testimonial Evidence   This message is similar to employing a spokesperson except instead of paid celebrities, the featured speaker is a typical user who has truly benefited from using the product.

Scientific Evidence   This message presents scientific or other types of evidence proving the marketer's claims.

FACTORS TO CONSIDER

While every message must be distinct, meaningful and credible, the marketer must consider other factors in their marketing plan. The marketer must decide the advertisement's *reach*, *frequency*, and *timing*. Reach measures in percentages, how much of the targeted audience was exposed to the advertisement over a period of time. Print and online media are the most cost effective, but television ads are more memorable. Frequency measures the amount of times a person is exposed to the message. Finally, the marketer must decide when to release the advertisement. It makes little sense to advertise an outdoor water-park. Timing is equally important as reach and frequency.

The power of advertising is limited by its impersonal nature and its inability to employ individualized persuasion techniques. There are a few exceptions, but advertising is a one-way communication process: it the marketer who tries to persuade the audience to act. Because the message is written for an audience, it is not as persuasive as an astute salesperson who can modify their sales pitch accordingly.

SALES PROMOTIONS

Sales promotions are short-term incentives to encourage customers to make a purchase. Sales promotions are popular with vendors because customers easily recognize the value a sales promotion offers: savings. What's more, sales promotions enable firms to shed excess inventory in their warehouses.

TYPES OF SALES PROMOTIONS:

Advertising specialties   A product imprinted with a logo or promotional message. Marketers frequently imprint the corporate logo on items such as mugs, tee shirts, and laptop bags for free to their employees and curious onlookers at recruitment fairs.

Cash rebates   A partial refund to the buyer.

Contests, sweepstakes and games   Sales promotion techniques where chance factors heavily in determining those eligible to receive the promotion.

Coupons   Printed certificates entitling the holder to receive the stated price reduction towards the purchase of a product.

Discounting   Reducing the listed price for a limited period of time

Loyalty programs   An incentive program offering non-cash benefits encouraging buyers to remain loyal to the marketer. Virtually every credit card company credits users with points that can be returned to receive products such as free airline tickets.

Point-of-purchase   Promotional materials placed at the point of purchase or sale. Large sized grocery stores often place an advertised item at the checkout counter.

Premiums   A product of value bundled for free or for a nominal fee to encourage a purchase. A favourite tactic of cereal companies is to include a free toy within each box.

Samples   A limited batch of the product dispensed to potential buyers.

FACTORS TO CONSIDER

When developing a sales promotion program, the marketer must make several decisions. First, he or she decides the extent of the savings offered to the customer. For the most part, consumers are sensitive to price changes in the short-term, therefore, incremental changes can significantly change sales revenue. The second issue to consider is to place limits on the length of the promotion. Long-standing sales promotions diminish the "act now" impulse. Even worse, if a product is heavily promoted for long periods of time, customers will expect the price reduction to endure. For more higher end brands there is real danger that if you promote more than once or twice a year you may damage the exclusivity of the brand. Some brands pride themselves on never being on sale. High-end department stores often limit themselves to two sales a year, after Christmas and in the summer. More than that and customers might start thinking they are buying at K-Mart or Woolworth's or some other lower end chain, heavens be!

PUBLIC RELATIONS

The primary role of public relations is to influence the public's beliefs, feelings and opinions about the company by placing information in the media without paying for the airtime or space consumed in the media. Typically, a public relations department circulates story ideas, press releases and other items of interest to media organizations in the hope the story is picked up by the media. Favourable stories reported in the media achieve the same effect as advertising, with the added bonus of being associated with the credibility of the media organization that circulated the information. And best of all, it's free since journalists cover the story. In short content trumps advertising in the credibility department. Public relations is a pull strategy.

PUBLIC RELATIONS TOOLS

Buzz marketing Capturing attention of customers and the media by creating a message that is newsworthy, entertaining or a topic of conversation. From time to time news stories appear in the media about some young males and their partners have dubbed drugs designed to combat erectile dysfunction as *"le weekend"*. More on this important topic below.

Guerilla marketing Grabbing the attention of consumers by creating seemingly impromptu promotional campaigns in public spaces where consumers engage in their daily routine. In every metropolitan region, marketers hand out free samples in crowded public spaces.

News reports Sending completed news reports to media organizations demonstrating the product's benefits

Press releases Creating news forms designed to attract the interest of the media to cover an event the marketer is sponsoring.

Public service activities Donating money, volunteers or resources to activities designed to support a social cause.

Special events A conference, presentation, or other type of organized event that tries to address an issue of public interest.

FACTORS TO CONSIDER

The aim of public relations is to create messages that build a favourable reputation for the company without paying the full cost of dissemination. Because the firm relies on the media and individuals to circulate the information, the firm loses control over how the message is transmitted; if the audience realizes the agenda behind the message, they can react negatively, rendering the message into a symbol of scorn or ridicule. Let's now turn to a bit more on buzz which is an increasingly important tool in the post-modern marketer's kit bag.

BUZZ MARKETING

As we discussed earlier, we live in an over communicated to age. The average Westerner is exposed to thousands of commercials' messages a day. It all adds up to too many messages chasing too little attention span. Tom Davenport, a well-known IT prof has famously said, "A few observant people have begun to argue that today's scarce resource – and thus the currency of the new economy – is actually attention". We think he is absolutely spot on. So how do we get through our over communicated, over advertised to market? One key answer is buzz marketing. Not a new idea but one that is gaining increasing street cred. Buzz marketing allows you to get in "under the radar".

Nowhere is truer than for the Nexters generation. For them, the most important influencers regarding spending in order of importance are friends, television, magazines, movies, the Internet and sports. Having seen more commercials than any generation before, the youngsters are advertising savvy and are hard to influence. Youngsters are sensitive when it comes to being marketed to. They want to discover the brand through underground channels, not classic ads. To break through the clutter, commercials need to be exceptionally original. Otherwise, flooding the air with GRPs (gross rating points – a way of measuring advertising spend) will only annoy the target market and damage both the brand and sales. Taking the creative approach pays handsomely. Brand preference builds at much younger ages than ever before. As teenagers have more disposable income than previous generations, their lifetime value is high if they remain loyal to the brand. Capturing this segment is crucial for the future of many companies. We have to ask ourselves, what can firms do to lure the reluctant youngsters to buy their products? Buzz seems to be one key way of going underneath their radar.

There is little research about buzz as it is a relatively new concept and scholars only recently started to explore the buzz generators and their effects. Buzz is formed by all the discussions regarding a brand, product, event and so on among people at any moment in time. What are some characteristics of the buzz? Some early lessons are emerging. First, buzz spreading cannot be controlled. It is spread exponentially through word of mouth, buzz can be generated, but cannot be moulded, directed, or stopped. Buzz is like a snowball which grows, gets momentum and finally melts if it is not refuelled. Second, the message cannot be controlled. The message is distorted and filtered by every transmitter and receptor of buzz. Its downside is that word of mouth can become negative, with important implications for the product or company that tries to generate buzz. To be effective, underground buzz must not be perceived as advertising by the target audience, as people will not transmit a commercial message. Therefore, companies need to pay attention not to mix classical advertising techniques with a buzz campaign, at least during the buzz building stage. Later, when the snowball starts rolling, traditional means can be used to reinforce and fuel the buzz.

Buzz cannot be targeted at a specific segment of population, but rather it spreads through a network of hubs and spokes. Buzz spreads across the borders at the light of email and chat rooms. At certain moments in time it affects clusters of customers and it rapidly migrates towards others crossing borders. A good way to control the word of mouth and to reinforce it would be to use endorsers placed in hubs. For example, teenagers gather in dance clubs, schools, and cafeterias and so on. By hiring opinion leaders – cool youngsters their peers look up to as endorsers of the brand, the brand becomes more visible and "cool by association". Procter & Gamble hires Tremor a company that sends products and coupons to 13–19-year-olds in its database. Lured by the chance to win products, the teenagers endorse products chosen by Tremor's clients.

Keeping the supply limited in the incipient stages of the process fuels the buzz and drives demand. Teenagers generally avoid main-stream products, so unique gear that "you've got to have" drives youngsters crazy. When the company launches the product in the mass markets, there is no need to build awareness as teenagers already know about the product. Few realize that by the time they buy it the product is mainstream. When the inevitable strikes them, they will rush to jump on the new latest trend and crave another new gear.

Buzz is one of the new kids of the block. There are few metrics to assess its success and power. However, the reality shows that word of mouth can transform overnight an anonymous product into a success story. In the future, most probably the media planning budget will include a position for the buzz marketing campaign. Until then we can only cross our fingers and hope that our advertising agency does not waste more than half of our advertising budget.

Table 5.1 Promotion Tool Kit

Advertising	Sales Promotion	Public Relations	Direct Marketing	Personal Selling
Banner ads	Contest sweepstakes	Annual reports	Catalogues	Incentive programs
Billboards	Coupons	Charitable donations	Internet	Meetings
Booklets	Exhibits	Community relations	E-mail	Presentations
Broadcast ads	Gifts		Fax	Samples
Brochures	Low-interest financing	Corporate magazines	Mail	Trade shows
Directories		Lobbying	Telemarketing	
Inner-Packaging	Product demonstrations	Media	TV shopping	
Leaflets	Rebates	Press kits	Voice mail	
Motion pictures	Sampling	Public events		
Outer-packaging	Tie-ins	Publications		
Pamphlets	Trade shows	Seminars		
Point of purchase displays	Trade-in allowances	Speeches		
Print ads		Sponsorships		
Shop displays				
Symbols and logos				
Videogames				

PERSONAL SELLING AND DIRECT MARKETING

Unlike the other three promotional tools personal selling and direct marketing are highly interactive experiences. Buyers and sellers are in constant communication with each other, with each party adjusting their message according to the other's specific needs. The other three promotional approaches are impersonal in nature: the firm releases the message, and tries to devise methods of increasing the chances of the audience absorbing the information. Since we discuss personal selling and direct marketing at the end of this chapter, we shall not discuss these two promotional tools at this point.

SUMMARY

- Marketers choose between employing a push or pull strategy to communicate to their customers. The strategy chosen depends heavily on the product.
- When the appropriate strategy is chosen, the manager must decide how best to measure success.
- Managers better get used to the idea that certain promotional tools do not account as neatly as they would like especially when evaluating the level of buzz surrounding a product.
- Measuring success should be secondary to the real goal of promotion, which is to send messages to the customer. Done properly, every message that the customer receives will be consistent.
- It is that consistency that marketers should aim for because with a consistent message, the customer eventually understands and retains what the product is and the benefits offered.

CRITICAL QUESTIONS

1   Review the five elements of the promotion mix. Discuss the advantages and disadvantages of advertising, sales promotions and public relations. If you were promoting a new product, which one or ones would you choose? Why?

2 What are the implications of media fragmentation for promoting consumer goods? Are the types of broadcasts changing to reflect this reality?

3 When supermodel Kate Moss was arrested for possession of cocaine, her sponsors immediately cancelled her contract to promote their product. Why did they do this? Does the hierarchy of effects model provide a good explanation?

4 How are brands affected by each promotional tool?

GLOSSARY

Advertising The placement of announcements and persuasive messages in time or space purchased in any of the mass media by business firms, non-profit organizations, government agencies, and individuals who seek to inform and/ or persuade members of a particular target market or audience about their products, services, organizations, or ideas.

Frequency The number of times a person is exposed to an advertisement.

Hierarchy of effects model A six-stage model tracing the steps a customer undergoes before making any purchasing decision.

Integrated Marketing Communication (IMC) A promotion strategy whereby all promotional activities are coordinated to ensure the consistency and quality of the transmitted message.

Media fragmentation A phenomenon whereby market forces are driving media channels to focus on a smaller and smaller sized audiences.

Personal selling A promotional tool where the marketer uses salespeople to convince interested buyers to spend.

Podcasts A free audio broadcast available for downloading onto portable listening devices or computers.

Promotion mix The blend of the five tools used by marketers to promote a product.

Public relations A promotional tool where the marketer attempts to influence public opinion by releasing one-sided information through news media channels.

Pull strategy A promotional strategy whereby the promotional mix is tailored to attract the target market, who in turn requests distribution channels to supply the product.

Push strategy   A promotional strategy whereby the promotional mix is tailored to push a product through various channels to the target market.

Reach   Measure of the effectiveness of an advertising campaign in percentages.

Sales promotions   Monetary incentives to make a purchase immediately.

Timing   Releasing an advertisement at a time that minimizes the risk of confusing the audience.

6

PEOPLE

Why have we included people as the final part of the marketing mix? Some consider personal selling as the interpersonal arm of the promotion mix. They regard employees as being a walking, talking, communication device that interacts with customers in order to inform them of the product offering. Characterizing people as an interactive billboard downplays their importance. Even in the modern economy where billions of goods and services are traded instantly, the human touch will always play a vital role in guiding the business process. For it is the relationship between buyer and seller, a relationship based on mutual interests, that creates the business opportunity for both parties to derive value and satisfaction. As Rolph Anderson, a business professor at Drexel University puts it, "[a person] responds to subtle clues, anticipates customer needs, provides personal service, nurtures on-going relationships and creates profitable new business strategies with their customers". People are more than just a two-way radio. People are the cement that binds customer value to satisfaction. Of course it is not just salespeople but flight attendants, barbers, lawyers, maids and many more that are all part of the experience of our product/service.

Thus in this chapter we look at three types of people involved in the exchange process between buyer and seller: salespeople, direct marketers and support staff.

The salesperson plays a special role in the exchange process. In most cases, he or she is the sole link between seller and buyer, which in effect means they serve both parties. For the customer, the salesperson is the official company representative. He or she will find and develop new business opportunities, negotiate the terms of the sales and follow-up once the sale is completed. At the same time, the salesperson adopts the role of advocate, relaying customer concerns and wants to the relevant department. When Karl was a young salesperson at IBM, one day his boss John Houlden asked him to pull out his paycheque. Somewhat mystified he complied, knowing a moral would shortly be delivered. He asked, "What is the name at the top?". He replied, "IBM". Following this his boss said, "Don't ever forget it." End of lesson. Houlden was reminding Karl he was in danger of falling into one of the traps a sales rep faces, that is, identifying with the customer so much so that they forget who they really work for.

SALES FORCE MANAGEMENT

Sales is a profession where individuals face high rejection rates, where they work in isolation and where they too often find themselves constantly travelling. As we stated in the first chapter, avoiding isolation and enhancing self-esteem are important determinants of human behaviour. Because the work conditions are antithetical to those activities there is an impression that successful salespeople must have an innate ability to sell. In other words, some are born to sell, others not. Selling is not genetic. Studies show that to succeed in sales, one must be a risk-taker, be resourceful, be able to empathize and be filled with a nearly unbounded reservoir of self-confidence. Every human possesses these qualities and traits, however, the degree to which they are developed varies from person to person. Managers must therefore develop strategies that enhance a person's selling skills and reinforce a person's sense of purpose. One of the most famous and well read sales motivation writers is Zig Ziglar. One of his key points is that a salesperson must learn to like hearing no. When you have heard seven nos, you know the next person will say yes. Statistically this is true. The first person has a 50% chance of saying no, the second has a 25% chance, the third, 12.5%. Halving the probability of rejection four more times will equal zero. This sounds particularly silly to most people but for many salespeople this actually makes sense.

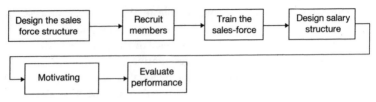

Figure 6.1 The Sales Force Management Model

We define **sales force management** as the analysis, planning, implementation, and control of all activities related to the sales force. These activities include crafting the structure of the sales department, delegating the tasks conducted by the salesperson, designing the selling strategies employed by the sales force and all actions related to recruiting, training, compensation and evaluation of the sales force. Figure 6.1 illustrates the sales force management model.

SALES FORCE STRUCTURE

A study published by Benson Shapiro and Stephen Doyle reported that salespeople whose tasks that were clearly articulated performed better than those that didn't. More surprisingly, the two concluded that sales-task clarity, as they called it, had a greater impact on employee motivation than the salary paid or the seller's personality. What managers can learn from Shapiro's and Doyle's study is that salespeople are more responsive to clarity than monetary incentives. Clearly defining the roles of sales force – or structure in management speak – increases the likelihood the salesperson acts in a manner congruent to the goals of the corporation, which is to build long-term relationships with customers through satisfying current, and anticipating future, needs.

TERRITORIAL SALES FORCE

The simplest method of dividing responsibilities is to devise a territorial sales force structure (TSF). To construct a TSF, the manager divides the region in which the target market resides into smaller units. One salesperson is assigned to each unit, bestowed with the exclusive right to promote the full product-line and maintain local business relationships. The company in turn creates ancillary support services including technical support, and customer service. In short, the salesperson sells, the company supports. From a customer-oriented perspective, there are three advantages of implementing a TSF structure. First, by assigning one salesperson to a particular region, thereby creating a mutual dependence between the salesperson and the customer, concerns raised by clients will be heard by a sympathetic ear. Second, it fosters higher customer satisfaction because the salesperson can devise product bundles tailored specifically to meet customer needs. Finally, by transferring the responsibility of support to the company, the customer receives assurances that technical and customer service related issues are handled by highly trained and competent staff whose primary task is to provide support. With a TSF, the argument goes, specialization breeds customer assurance.

The belief that specialization will always breed customer assurance is unfortunately idealistic. Granting exclusivity to the salesperson can hinder the process of building customer relationships because there are no checks to see if the salesperson is making reasonable attempts at finding new customers. But who can blame the salesperson for not wanting to solicit new business? With the constant travelling, low success rates and the salary correlated to performance, it is natural to avoid such stress once a stable client base is secured. Finally, if the product-line is diverse or highly technical in nature, unless properly trained, the salesperson will have difficulty communicating the benefits of each product of the product-line to potential customers.

PRODUCT SALES FORCE

For companies that sell a myriad of products in numerous markets, or for companies that manufacture products highly technical in nature, a product sales force structure (PSF) is more appropriate. This structure entails dividing the sales force along or a portion of the product-line, in effect transforming the salesperson into a product specialist. Specialization allows the salesperson to develop a fluency with the product's benefits, which is articulated to customers. A second advantage of becoming a product specialist is that because the salesperson understands all of the technical benefits and limitations of the product, they can quickly spot unmet customer needs and wants and suggest solutions. Sales forces that work like this include many in the high-tech industry and many B2B sales forces. The in-depth knowledge of a particular product and associated application is quite powerful.

Though the product sales force structure overcomes the inherent disadvantages of employing a territorial sales force structure, there are intrinsic problems. First, creating an army of specialists may actually lead to missed sales opportunities because the specialist is not aware of the benefits offered by other products sold by the business. There is an old saying, "if all you have is a hammer, everything looks like a nail". One of the advantages of a firm with a broad product-line, like HP or IBM, is that they can argue that they bring the proper tool to solve your problem, because they have a big bag of tools while a smaller firm has only one solution and that is what they will sell. Firms may also miss opportunities for additional sales because of sales myopia which naturally occurs when you are focused on one product. A sales rep who sells to just one customer or one industry gains tremendous knowledge of that firm and/or industry and can often go out into the bowels of the firm to find new applications and needs for their firms products, effectively stirring up additional business that otherwise would lay dormant. They also can develop in-depth relationships which are extremely helpful when problems occur, as they will in any firm, both sides have invested in the relationship and are more apt to be patient, it is more like a marriage than a one night stand.

The second disadvantage is related to the first. Bundling products often offers more value to customers than buying the products outright. However, bundling becomes more difficult because it requires coordination between the two sellers, not any easy thing to accomplish. One recent trend which many still find perplexing is that firms are competitors in the morning and then work together as partners in the afternoon. This leads to some confusion as to how to treat them and is an area we are still mucking about with.

CUSTOMER SALES FORCE

For those businesses which sell specialized products or services, a customer sales force structure (CSF) would be more appropriate.

Under CSF, resources are divided according to the client's importance; the more sales a buyer accounts for, the more resources there are dedicated to satisfying customer needs. Call it "spend to make". Because specialized products or services are customized, the sales force needed must be adept at understanding their client's core businesses. Investment bankers for example, are customer sales force agents. They understand how market dynamics affect their client's core business, and by offering a variety of products to strengthen those competencies, the salesperson gains a deep understanding of the strengths and weaknesses of their client's company. Learning their client's deepest secrets allows the sale agent to quickly identify and propose new business opportunities. A customer sales force is advantageous because the salesperson or team becomes the sole point of contact. What's more, a CSF allows the client to focus their efforts on managing the day-to-day affairs of the company, not dedicating resources to assess future threats, opportunities and weaknesses.

The most serious drawback of a customer sales force model is that as the deals grow in value, a dependency issue is created. For example, the accounting department of Arthur Andersen, the auditor of the now bankrupt energy trader Enron, was supposed to conduct independent audits of Enron's financial statements. Auditing however is a low-margin business. At the same time, Enron was purchasing high-margin consulting services from another division of Arthur Andersen, creating a potential conflict of interest. Did Arthur Anderson's auditors knowingly overlook the warning signs in order to ensure their company still received those lucrative consulting contracts? We'll never know for certain. The Supreme Court of the United States has since cleared Arthur Andersen of any wrongdoing in the collapse of Enron. However, the price paid for even being associated with the scandal was significant, if not fatal: from a high of 85,000 employees worldwide, the company now employs about 200 people, mostly lawyers who are busy dealing with the other 100 or more civil suits that are still pending.

HYBRID SALES FORCE

For companies that sell a wide range of products over a wide geographical region to many customers strictly employing one of the sales force models places unnecessary restriction on the company. As such, companies often employ a hybrid structure to offset some of the more glaring disadvantages. This approach is often used on a global basis where you will organize the sales force in different ways in different countries depending on the maturity of the market, the length of time you have been in the market and how competitors do business in that country. This is less of a problem than you might think if your customer buys primarily in the country they are headquartered in, which is true for many firms. However, if your customers are global multinationals and buy on a global basis this may require that you have a global account manager whose responsibilities cut across countries; this leads to territorial disputes and other assorted joys but an increasing number of customer are demanding it, more on this later on the chapter on international and global marketing. No matter which model is chosen, there will always be disadvantages since each company's needs are different. Therefore, each company should select a structure that fits with their overall marketing strategy and where the salesperson's duties are clearly defined.

SALES FORCE SIZE

Having chosen the appropriate structure, the next step is to estimate the size of the sales force. One method is to use a **workload approach** to set the sales force size. With this approach, a company determines the number of calls needed to be made each year to maintain an existing client base. To do so, the company first groups their clients into a number of classes. The filtering criteria could be volume, customer size, account status, location, or any other variable by which the seller evaluates their operations. Suppose there are three classes of customers: A, B and C. There are 1000 type A accounts, 500 type B accounts and 100 type C accounts. Type A accounts require 20 calls a year. Type B accounts require 30, whereas type C accounts require 5 calls a year. The sales force's workload is the number of calls needed to make in one year would be [(1000 x 20) + (500 x 30) + (100 x 5)] or 35,500 calls. Suppose each salesperson makes 250 calls a year, the company would then need 142 people (35,500 / 250).

RECRUITING AND SELECTING SALESPEOPLE

We stated earlier that successful salespeople must be risk-takers, be resourceful, be self-confident and be able to empathize with others. Finding individuals with these characteristics can lead to dramatic changes to the balance sheet. Studies have shown on *average*, just 30% of the sales force accounts for 60% of a company's revenue. A star salesperson shines.

Because companies are looking for particular characteristics in their sales force, often multiple interviews are needed before the company decides to make an employment offer. Many companies also require candidates to write aptitude tests, measuring their intelligence quotient, analytical and organizational abilities, personality traits, and a host of other factors. One need not fret too much about aptitude tests. While there is evidence suggesting high-test scores predict future sales performance, the correlation between the two is debatable. Past employment history, reference letters and interviewer reactions are just as good if not better indicators of future performance. Salespeople simply sell, looking at their track record is quite important.

TRAINING SALESPEOPLE

The third step in the model is to train the sales force. Training provides the salesperson with information that not only includes details about the products that they will be selling, but also facts regarding the habits of the target market, and customer need. Training also includes an explanation of the salesperson's responsibilities and duties, and the personal selling process, which we will explain in depth later in the chapter. Finally, a well-designed training program will also include details on competitor strategies, the company's mission, financial structure, organization and corporate objectives. For brand sales reps, training around the professional sales call as discussed shortly is critical. Some firms are known as providing great sales training, Xerox for example, and young people wanting a career in sales are well advised to start off with one of these firms to get the basics down right as a great foundation to a career in sales.

COMPENSATING PEOPLE

Due to the physical and mental demands placed on a salesperson, those aspects must be reflected in the compensation package offered to the salesperson. Depending on the working conditions, the salary could be simply a fixed salary, or a salary plus commission or a salary plus bonuses. Management must decide on which combination or mix will motivate the salesperson and focus their activities to realize the corporation's objectives.

MOTIVATING SALESPEOPLE

Due to the day-to-day stress placed on the salesperson, morale can quickly plummet. Astute managers can boost morale and consequently boost performance through a combination of repeated usage of positive reinforcement, changing the compensation structure, to improve the sense of commitment the salesperson has to the company. For many salespeople compensation, that is to say money, is big motivator, though to be honest often it is more as a marker of success as opposed to the money itself. At IBM the sales force would largely act like a school of fish that moves as if one, when we heard there was a bonus for a particular product we would all go out and try very hard to sell that particular product. At a deeper level this suggests that many salespeople have a particularly high need for achievement and just find pleasure in the act of succeeding on a regular basis.

EVALUATING SALESPEOPLE

While the simplest way to evaluate a salesperson is to compare their sales results with the metrics utilized to evaluate performance, how does a manager evaluate a salesperson during the selling process?

One method is to receive progress reports from each salesperson, detailing their completed activities, calls they've made, expenses they've accrued to date. With this information the manager remains informed as to which companies have been contacted, and the status of each account. The manager now has at his or her disposal the needed information to compare the progress of each account, and can intervene directly if a sale is taking too long to close. In sales, results are the ultimate long-term measure.

THE SELLING PROCESS

We now turn to the selling process, a methodology that the sales-person follows in order to close a sale. The personal selling process consists of seven parts: prospecting, pre-approaching, approaching, the sales call, closing (part of the sales call) and following up.

PROSPECTING

The first step in the selling process is called **prospecting**. Prospecting involves devising a list of qualified customers who would be receptive to a marketing offer, at this point they are merely suspects. Finding the right customers saves resources and avoids the possibility of building a client base whose needs and wants are difficult to satisfy.

Although the company can provide leads on prospective sales opportunities, capable salespeople generate new business by themselves. Asking existing clients for referrals, trolling telephone directories and searching the Internet are just some of the methods one can use to find the names and contact information of potential clients. The truly bold salesperson engages in a practice known as **cold-calling**, which involves calling or visiting the offices of a prospect unannounced. This is psychologically challenging. Salespeople spend months calling hundred of firms; most lead to nothing. We have a name for salespeople that thrive in this hothouse atmosphere, hunters. They are in contrast to farmers who prefer to work with existing customers and till them to get additional business for their firms. Both are valuable but generally hunters are more rare and are paid more because of the value of brand new customers and the sheer difficulty of bringing them in. Once a list of potential customers has been drawn up, the sales-person must screen out those that offer the least potential. You may wish to picture a funnel, at the wide end is a large number of suspects at the narrow bit there is relatively small number of customers who actually buy substantially. The job of sales is to turn the large majority of suspects into customers, along the way a salesperson qualifies who should move to the next phase of the funnel. The further down the funnel you get the more expensive it is. Only customers who are really interested should be allowed to move the next level of higher marketing spend. Once again, we make the point that marketing dollars, pounds, euros and yen should only be spent on those who have a high potential to get to the next part of the funnel and ultimately to become loyal repeat profitable customers. Learning this type of discipline is one of the hardest lessons for budding marketers.

PRE-APPROACHING

Having established a list of qualified customers, the salesperson then starts the second stage of the selling process, which is called the pre-approach. The pre-approach stage entails researching information about the prospect: What are their needs? How large is the company? Who are their existing suppliers? Who is the person (or people) that approves a purchase? To learn about the prospective client, the salesperson can consult their personal contacts, industry and online sources, and analysts.

APPROACHING

Armed with enough background information, the seller can devise a sales strategy as to which method is best to approach the prospective client. The seller should decide if a letter or a phone call will be sufficient, or if a personal visit is needed to begin a relationship. First impressions are vitally important in building goodwill between the two parties. The more favourable impression the seller makes, the more favourable the buyer will be to make a purchase.

The next three parts, presenting, objection handling and closing can best be summarized as part of a professional sales call.

THE PROFESSIONAL SALES CALL

When done well a professional sales call is a pleasure for a customer. A key starting point is to realize that most salespeople spend much too much time talking and nowhere near enough time listening. When you think of the typical used car or electronics store salesperson we cannot help but think of them as a non-stop talker, this is exactly wrong. On average an excellent salesperson spends more like 75% of their time listening and 25% of their time selling their product. Keeping this in mind let's go through a professional sales call.

The starting portion of a sales call is a critical bit and one not to be short-changed. It is the rapport building stage. The fundamental thought is that people buy from people they like, now that does not mean that you can cheat them, offer them a terrible price or otherwise not be on the ball. But it is a fundamental truth for the vast majority of human beings, buying is a social and emotional process. For most buyers sitting and having a coffee or other culturally relevant beverage and having a pleasant chat about football (US or the rest-of-the-world type), or baseball or cricket or what have you, is quite a nice change in their day. Most great salespeople learn to ask for a coffee or water in order to make room for social chit chat with the customer or potential customer as a way of building the start of the relationship of trust and liking. Indeed in the Middle East drinking a warm coffee or tea is essential because it is considered good manners. For someone you have not met before this also critical because during the first five minutes, people's impressions are being formed; if it is a pleasant and positive one that positive image will remain for a long time. This human-to-human exchange will last at least a few minutes, a good salesperson engages in light chit-chat and treats small talk as an important skill. Almost always the customer will signal when it is over and it is time to move onto business. They do this by clearing their throats and falling silent, by picking up a file from their desk and straightening it, or by saying explicitly, "let's now do our business", though in slightly less direct words. A few customers will allow the rapport stage to go on forever if you let them. A wise salesperson will themselves end this part of the sales call eventually by saying, with considerable reluctance in their voice, "I would love nothing better than to chat about Man United all day . . . but my boss" and then shrug their shoulders to show that they sadly must talk about business.

The next phase is a brief one, here the salesperson gives their **Initial Benefit Statement** (IBS). The IBS is a short statement saying why you are there and asking the person if that is of interest. Why you ask if your visit is of interest is to get their permission to continue. We will do this throughout the sales call. It is similar to tacking a hallway carpet. If you just drop a carpet down in a hallway and randomly tack here and there what you will have is a carpet that is a mass of waves, bits sticking up and generally something that looks a right mess. The proper way to end with a nice flat well laid carpet is to carefully tack down the first foot or two and then move onto tack down the next few feet and so on down to the end of the hall. A good sales call is similar. You want the customer to feel that each step of the call is a next logical step, that is not a reach but rather is perfectly sensible, they don't feel manipulated but are rather in full agreement with the salesperson. We will check back with the customer throughout our professional sales call. After the customer has agreed that why you are there is relevant for them you then move to the next phase. If the customer doesn't agree that what you are there to discuss is for them, you then question and find out why. You will often find that it is just a misunderstanding; once you clear that up you may proceed but sometimes you may find that you are meeting with the wrong person. In that case you ask them who is the right person for you to see, thank them for their time and head off to find the right person, thankful that you have not wasted their time any more and more fundamentally that you have not wasted any more of your most precious resource – your sales time! We call this permission marketing.

At this point many salespeople would launch into their sales pitch. Outstanding salespeople realize that you should next move into the heart of the sales call, questioning the customer about their needs. This will often take up the majority of the time of the sales call. During this phase the salesperson asks the customer about how they are solving the problem that he/she wants to address with their product today. This interested probing will allow the salesperson to understand the context of the customer and what is important to them. This will go on for 15, 20, 30 minutes or more depending on the customer and the topic. At the end of the questioning stage the salesperson will then summarize what they have learned. This will encourage the customer that you have actually listened (an unusual thing for most of us and rather enjoyable) and then you check back with them that you have accurately reflected your discussion. A good question to ask is did I get your priorities of needs right? This gives the customer the chance to add anything that they think you have missed and also implicitly asks permission to then move to the next phase. In the next phase, the product presentation, the salesperson talks, finally, about their product. But not in a canned presentation for the "generic" average customer but absolutely adjusted to fit the needs, requirements and real world of the customer. This approach harnesses the great power of a sales rep which an ad, brochure or CD cannot do, that is tailor your presentation to them.

During the product presentation or discussion the sales rep should make sure that they present benefits not features. Features are things about the product which the company cares about, the speed of the central processor for a computer company, the strength of signal of cellphone, where what the customer cares about how fast they can work, if they can get a call at their cottage. In B2B marketing a key question you should be able to answer is how your product/service will allow the customer to be more profitable, that is have a better business, does it save them money, does it allow them to get additional revenue, retain key employees, these are the types of benefits businesses are looking for.

After you have presented the key benefits of your product based on what you had learned earlier in the questioning phase you then summarize the key benefits of your product and how that will help your customer address some of their critical issues. If it does not address critical issues why should they bother? This is even truer the higher you get in an organization. In most organizations, business or public sector, the larger the amount you are asking the organization to spend the higher up you have to go to get permission to spend. This is called signing authority. A first level manager might be able to spend $10,000 without permission from their manager, but over that they must have the signature of their manager. This means that their manager is someone who is a key decision maker whom the salesperson must reach and convince of the value of their product. For larger ticket items, $100,000 you may well have to go to a third or fourth level manager, again the number of players you have to influence grows. For a very large sale, $1,000,000 or more for a medium size company or perhaps $100,000,000 for very large firm you must go to the CEO and in some cases to the board of directors. Bombardier, the third largest commercial aircraft maker in the world has recently launched a new series of aircraft called the C-series which is a plane series of 100–130 passengers. They will spend over $2 billion at minimum and 5 years to bring this plane to market. The board of directors met several times before they gave their go ahead to the project.

A key thought here is that the larger the ticket price the more complex the sale becomes. This introduces the idea of a **buying centre**. In some organizations one person makes the decision and is the only influence on the sales. In many B2B sales it is much more complex than that. Multiple players with multiple agendas influence the final decision, depending as noted above the size and strategic importance of the deal. Often four key roles can be identified. The **decision maker** who actually decides but is influenced by others and so does not decide on his/her own. Influencers are people who don't decide but have important input to the decision. Financial people may have input in terms of the impact of the deal on the organization's cash flow or ability to improve profitability. User managers will undoubtedly have an opinion on whether the new equipment is easier to work with than the older generation of equipment. Technical people often act as **gatekeepers** who get to say who you may buy from based on an approved set of vendors but cannot insist on one above another. Finally senior executives may take a different view based on the strategy of the organization, almost always strategy trumps the thinking of people lower in the organization. The task of the sales rep is clear, make sure they understand the varying agendas of each key influencer and tailor their approach to align their product with the **agenda** of each of those key players. Easier said than done but quite critical.

During the sales call the customer will generally have objections in their mind. Throughout the presentation, the salesperson should be ready to answer whatever queries or objections the customer might have. This is called **objection handling**. Having a well-trained and knowledgeable staff improves the salesperson's ability in handling. The salesperson should also probe the customer from time to time, when they look quizzical or confused by what we are saying. If an objection lays unaddressed in the customer's mind we have left a seed which will almost certainly germinate into a deal killer, that is why good salespeople are quite happy to hear objections. It is better that you hear them and deal with them than they are left unanswered. A sales force team should get together from time to time to hold an objection clinic where they can rehearse good answers to the objections that they will hear from potential customers. If you hear a new objection that you don't have an answer to the best course is to cheerfully admit that and tell the customer that you will get back them later. Honesty really is the best policy, otherwise you will get in trouble and hurt that most valuable thing, trust.

CLOSING

Once all of the prospect's objections have been dealt with, the salesperson attempts to close the sale by asking for an order. Though most people find that rather intimidating it generally comes as no surprise to the customer, they expect salespeople to ask for the order and are not upset when you do. If you have made a logic sales call it should naturally flow from the conversation you have been having. For many sales an order will not result from the first call, but every sales call should have an objective, an ambitious but realistic target. For example, to obtain permission to call on another person in the buying centre, to visit a customer reference site or that you return with some financial analysis done which you will then jointly review. However, the moment of truth will hopefully arrive – asking for that valuable thing, the point of the salesperson's business life, the order.

Knowing when to close the sale is more of an art then a science. Slight nods of the head, the types of comments and questions from the prospect are subtle but telling clues as to the seriousness of the buyer. Once the salesperson feels the time is right to close, there are a number of techniques they can employ. They can fill out an order for the prospect, remind the buyer that waiting will likely mean they will lose the order, or offer incentives, such as a lower price, or extra quantities. The aim is to instil a sense of urgency in the buyer's mind to make a purchase immediately.

FOLLOWING-UP

The last step in the selling process is the **follow-up**. The follow-up is essential to the selling process if the salesperson wants to retain the customer for future business. Following-up entails contacting the client, asking them for feedback regarding their order.

DIRECT MARKETING

One of the fastest growing segments in the marketing industry is the direct marketing industry. We define **direct marketing** as a marketing strategy to build stronger, more personal relationships between the buyer and selected customers directly. In other words, there are no intermediary promotion or distribution channels between the buyer and seller. Direct marketing entails providing a marketing offer specifically tailored to the needs or wants of a narrowly defined segment. If the offer is flexible enough, it is theoretically possible to capture the entire consumer surplus with a direct marketing strategy; individuals receive exactly what they want. To offer such products, direct marketers need large databases containing information on their customers, information that includes demographic, psychographic, geographic and behavioural data. Using statistics, analysts uncover similar preferences between dissimilar customers, enabling the direct marketer to craft a marketing offer to the under-served segment. Direct marketing deepens the relationship between buyer and seller.

Direct marketing is by no means a new phenomenon. The retailing giant Sears Roebuck started as a catalogue company over 100 years ago. Sears became a success because they directly interacted with the customer, always fulfilling their marketing offer, which was to deliver affordable clothing to the customer's home in a timely fashion.

BENEFITS OF DIRECT MARKETING

Employing a direct marketing model offers many benefits to buyers and sellers. For the buyers, direct marketing is a quick, and convenient means of purchasing goods they want. Direct marketing also facilitates the possibility of customizing the order, therefore the buyers receive the product they want, not the product marketers think they want. For sellers, direct marketing is also beneficial. By offering consumers products that they want, the seller can capture more of the consumer surplus. Second, by directly contacting the consumer, the marketer does not need to build a retail presence to reach customers. Third, direct marketing allows the marketer to craft marketing offers specifically targeted to a small group or even an individual buyer.

FORMS OF DIRECT MARKETING

There are seven forms of direct marketing: personal selling, online marketing, telephone marketing, direct-mail marketing, catalogue marketing, direct-response television marketing, and kiosk marketing. We take a look at a few.

TELEPHONE MARKETING

Telephone marketing is a cost-effective way of reaching a customer relative to conventional channels. In previous chapters we've demonstrated the high cost and difficulty of getting a message through to a customer, whereas only those that wish to be undisturbed will ignore a ringing telephone. Also, the cost of setting up a telephone marketing operation is considerably lower than advertising in the media. Buying a 60 second advertisement slot on a major network can cost hundreds of thousands of dollars, whereas the direct marketer only needs a toll-free telephone number. With a toll-free number, the marketer gains access to the entire region where the number services. By offering customers the chance to make a purchase immediately, is it any wonder why telephone marketing is one of the most popular forms of direct marketing, accounting for almost 35% of all direct marketing sales?

DIRECT MAIL MARKETING

Direct-mail marketing is the second most popular form of direct marketing, accounting for 30% of all direct marketing sales. Direct-mail marketing entails sending a marketing offer to a prospective customer residing in a particular geographic region. Messages can travel through the mail, Internet or through the telephone system in the form of a fax or voicemail. Whichever medium is chosen, the message sent to the customer will be customized to their wants, as determined by the database that contains their information. A critical success factor is the quality of the mailing list; firms exist which provide, for a price, mailing lists, though the quality of their lists varies. Though many people in the developed world don't like direct mail and trash virtually all they receive, for the right person at the right time the right direct mail piece is right on. For example, if you are a big fan of golf club making, you love to get direct mail about golf club making equipment. The lesson, find the right person and you can make a sale with direct mail.

Catalogue marketing is the third most popular form of direct marketing. Accounting for almost $200 billion in worldwide sales, catalogue marketing is similar to direct mail marketing with one notable exception: unlike in direct-mail marketing where the person contacted is a *prospective* customer, in catalogue marketing the seller already knows the buyer is interested. Visitors to the Sears department store, volunteer their mailing address in order to receive the catalogue. LL Bean is a Maine based company which has done extremely well not only in North America but enjoying considerable success in the UK as well as Britons get used to the idea of ordering something that they cannot see. In this type of market a strong brand which has the consumer's trust is extremely helpful. Dell, Neiman Marcus and General Electric are all examples of big, prestigious firms which have used catalogue marketing with considerable success.

DIRECT-RESPONSE TELEVISION MARKETING

Just as there's a telephone in nearly every home, the same can be said about the television set. As such, it didn't take long for marketers to start devising means of connecting to customers through the airwaves. What emerged was direct-response television marketing.

There are two forms of direct television marketing. The first is the infomercial, the second is cable television shopping. The infomercial is a 60 to 90 minute staged demonstration of the advertised product. Viewers watch how the product fares when subjected to a number of field tests. Other infomercials which late-night television watchers may recognize, suggest if one were to call at that moment, the somewhat attractive member of the opposite sex seen on the screen will be sitting on the other end of the telephone. Despite their seemingly comical advertisements, consumers in the US spend $2 billion each year on products advertised on television.

The second form of direct television marketing is cable television shopping. In this form, the advertiser obtains a broadcast license and promotes a wide range of products 24 hours a day. Advertisers pay the content provider a fee to list their product at the time when their target market will be watching. Like the infomercial, cable television shopping channels bring in billions.

KIOSK MARKETING

The final method of direct marketing is called kiosk marketing. Kiosk marketing entails placing a mobile stand in a place where the customer is most likely to be. The kiosk may be manned by one or two people, or could simply be a touch screen that displays information. The level of interaction between customer and seller in kiosk marketing is generally low because they are used primarily to gather or disseminate information. Examples of kiosks include, Eddie Bauer stores where customers can order from the entire line of products some of which are not available in the retail store and Florsheim Shoe kiosks placed in airports for home or office delivery. Our bank's ATMs placed in many and high traffic areas are another example.

PRIVACY ISSUES

Critics of direct marketing agree there are many advantages to creating relationships directly between the buyer and seller. However, they believe the cost to society is greater than those realized. Because companies understand the importance of retaining customers for the long-term, direct marketers are especially aggressive in targeting impulse or less-sophisticated clients: dinner time phone calls, nearly deafening television commercials advertising incredulous savings, or claims of large prizes awaiting. Furthermore, the amount of waste direct marketing generates is considerable. Too often consumers throw promotional material into the garbage, fed up with their mailboxes being stuffed full with advertisements. A lot of trees were cut down for no benefit to society. The aggressive and sometimes illegal tactics some direct marketers employ damage the reputation of the entire industry.

Critics are also concerned that with the rapidly declining cost of data-storage technologies, the consumer's right to privacy is under threat. With the notable exceptions of Europe and Canada, companies can use information they gathered from consumers in any means they see fit; it could be used by another department, sold to another company or given to a government agency. Direct marketing offers many advantages, however, the need to regulate the industry to balance privacy rights and commerce is clearly needed.

SUPPORT STAFF

Employing a well-trained and knowledgeable sales force, or employing a direct marketing strategy will build customer value and satisfaction. A third way to build customer value and satisfaction is by employing a well-trained and knowledgeable support staff whose activities are designed around satisfying customers. Take the airline industry for example. Before boarding a plane, the traveller presents their boarding pass to the checkout counter, is seated by an air-steward, is taken to their destination by a pilot, and finally receives their bags placed on the carousel by baggage handlers. Though the consumer may not be aware of the "behind the scenes" activities when they are working well, they certainly will notice when mistakes are made. This is one of the biggest areas for airlines to differentiate themselves from competitors in a way highly relevant to customers.

At the core of the people is the simple idea that all our marketing noise boils down to how people, our employees, treat our customers. If we have a bad experience all the marketing and advertising in the world don't amount to a hill of beans. It is how we are treated at the essential points of human contact that we judge a service business. A critical point is that more and more businesses are dominated by their services element, whether it is IBM or GE, both formally dominated by the manufacturing part of their business but now quite depend on services and their high profit margins.

We measure an airline to large degree by our experience when we call the airline frequent flyer program, at the business class lounge, with the flight attendants, with the ground service staff and with even the pilots. These are called "moments of truth", when the marketing efforts of BA or Southwestern are seen as hype or true. Interestingly the expression "moments of truth" was first widely used in the airline industry, by SAS. Based in Scandinavia, among the least hierarchical countries on earth, SAS had a real problem because in those type of societies service was not seen as a natural activity. It was only through a dint of long and hard work did they make service part of their corporate culture. Our people are profoundly in a services and increasingly experiential based economy. This is an important thing for marketers to focus on in the next 5 years.

SUMMARY

- Salespeople, direct marketers and support staff are the building blocks of a customer value and satisfaction strategy.
- Depending on their roles and responsibilities, the sales-person will be the sole point of contact with the client.
- Due to the high costs of employing a sales force, a system of sales management is required.
- There are six steps in a sales force management system: designing the appropriate structure, recruiting the right individuals, training the staff, developing the appropriate compensation structure, and evaluating results.
- Part of the training a salesperson receives is learning the seven steps of the selling process.
- Direct marketing creates direct connections to the consumer, offering them convenience and customized products.
- There are seven forms of direct marketing: personal selling, online marketing, telephone marketing, direct-mail marketing, catalogue marketing, direct response television marketing, and kiosk marketing.

CRITICAL QUESTIONS

1   What are the different types of sales force structures? What are the advantages and disadvantages?
2   How do people create an experience for the customer?
3   Pretend you're trying to sell lemonade to a customer. Trace the steps a customer goes through using the selling

process model. Could a few steps be skipped? Now pretend you're trying to sell a multimillion Euro piece of equipment. Are there noticeable differences in how you treat your customers? Why?

4   Discuss the various types of direct marketing. As the media channels continue to fragment into smaller channels, what effect will it have on direct marketers? Should they be regulated?

SUGGESTIONS FOR FURTHER READING

Christopher Lovelock, *Services Marketing: People, Technology, Strategy*, New Jersey, Prentice Hall, 2000.

One of the standard books in the area of services marketing with a real focus on people and how they deliver on your customer promise.

John Batson and Douglas Hoffman, *Managing Service Marketing*, Fort Worth, Texas: Dryden, 1999.

One of the best textbooks on service marketing, showing the difference and similarities to "traditional" marketing of tangible products.

GLOSSARY

Agenda   The goal an individual wishes to accomplish.

Approaching   The first meeting with a prospect.

Buying centre   A word describing the complex system that emerges from decentralizing the authority to buy an expensive product from one person to many people.

Catalogue marketing   A form of direct marketing where the seller sends a marketing offer to an interested buyer.

Closing   The step in the selling process where the salesperson requests the prospect places an order.

Cold-calling   A euphemism meaning calling on the telephone or visiting in person the prospect unannounced.

Customer sales force   A sales force structure where each salesperson specializes in selling to specific customers or industries.

Decision maker   The person(s) who has the authority to make a purchasing decision.

Direct-mail marketing   A form of direct marketing where the seller sends a marketing offer to a prospective customer through the mail, or through the telephone system in the form of a fax, or voicemail.

Direct marketing   A marketing strategy tailored around offering convenience, which in turn, builds stronger, more personal relationships between the buyer and selected customers. No intermediary promotion or distribution channels exist.

Direct-response television marketing   A form of direct marketing whereby the seller connects to a prospect through the airwaves, either by broadcasting an infomercial, or by advertising their product on a cable-shopping channel.

Following-up   The final step in the selling process where the salesperson contacts the prospect after completing sale ensuring the customer is satisfied with the product.

Gatekeepers   The individual(s) who recommends a list of vendors who sell products that could be of use to solve a company's needs.

Handling   The step in the selling process whereby the salesperson answers the prospect's questions or objections.

Initial brief statement   A brief that explains your business interests with another party.

Kiosk marketing   Placing mobile stands to disseminate corporate information or to collect contact information about a target market.

Objection handling   Having prepared answers to client questions or concerns.

Pre-approaching   Researching information about the prospect's needs and concerns.

Presenting   The step in the selling process in which the salesperson pitches the product to the prospect, highlighting the product's benefits.

Product sales force   A sales force structure where each salesperson specializes in selling a portion of the product-line.

Prospecting   Devising a list of qualified customers who would be receptive to a marketing offer.

Sales force management   The analysis, planning, implementation, and control of all activities related to the sales force. These activities include crafting the structure of the sales department, delegating the tasks conducted by the salesperson, designing the selling strategies employed by the sales force and all actions related to recruiting, training, compensation and evaluation of the sales force.

Sales-task clarity A set of clearly defined responsibilities and expectations for a salesperson.

Telephone marketing A form of direct marketing where the seller uses the telephone to contact customers.

Territorial sales force A sales force structure where each sales-person is assigned an exclusive geographical territory to sell the company's entire product-line.

Workload approach A model that evaluates the total amount of resources used to perform a task.

7

SEGMENTATION, TARGETING AND POSITIONING

MARKET SEGMENTATION

A large, heterogeneous market, is comprised of smaller groups with homogeneous preferences. **Market segmentation** is the practice of dividing a large heterogeneous market into smaller subgroups with shared characteristics in order to deliver a market offering that satisfies unmet needs as closely as possible. Since those within a segment have similar characteristics, marketers have found they respond similarly to a marketing strategy promoting a given product, at a certain price that is distributed in a particular fashion.

A central idea is that you can adjust the five levers of the marketing mix (our friends the 5 Ps) to more carefully align with the things that that segment or group prefer in your product class. This makes the product more suited to their needs than a generic product for the "average consumer". However, there is a cost, the cost of doing so. Every time you move the levers of the marketing mix one notch it adds cost and effort, so you do so only if you can earn additional revenue that outweighs any incurred cost. Let us give you an example of how clothing stores go after two different segments. A teenage girl's clothing shop plays music attractive to them, parents reaction is, "they call that music?", the teen sales-person is wearing braces and chewing gum, which looks on principle dangerous! A parent's job is to sit on a bench outside in the mall, reading the newspaper, drinking a cappuccino and yelling into the shop every ten minutes or so, "it's too short!", thinking this is generally wise advice for their teenage daughter. A clothing shop for her father is quite different. They are playing classic music or light jazz in the background, you can hear yourself think, they provide a cappuccino, the woods are dark and the lights are pleasantly muted, when the tailor measures you for a suit, he says, "Sir, I can see you have had a prosperous year", meaning you have put weight on, but he knows how to put it in the best possible light. Each shop is tailored to their respective segment and the target segment of the other is frankly a bit put off by the other's shop environment. This adjusting the marketing mix costs money, both are more expensive than a "cheap and cheerful" clothing department of Wal-Mart or Woolys. We only take on board this cost when we can make money from it.

In order to be classified as a market segment, it must have the following six characteristics:

- Homogeneity: The segment must share at least one variable in common.
- Measurable: The size, purchasing power and characteristics of the segment can be determined.
- Substantial: The segment must be large enough to yield an economic profit.
- Accessible: The segment must be easy to distribute to and serve after-sales support.
- Differentiable: The segment must react differently to a marketing mix than another segment.
- Actionable: The segment must respond to programs that are tailored to attract them.

Now that we have discussed what is market segment, we now move the discussion to how one segments a market.

SEGMENTING CONSUMER MARKETS

There are many ways of segmenting consumer markets, as a consumer you are familiar with many of them, let us list a few of the major ways.

GEOGRAPHIC SEGMENTATION

Geographic segmentation entails dividing the market into smaller geographical units. These units can represent nations, provinces, counties, cities, neighbourhoods, streets and even individual addresses. There are firms in the US, Canada, the UK and other countries that will sell you data based on census data at the level of a postal code. In Canada this means a few houses or an apartment building, a rather narrow focus. Geographic segmentation provides companies with the opportunity to tailor their products to suit the tastes and preferences of a unique region. In the Basque regions of Spain, residents speak Catalan as their first language, not Spanish. They also are fiercely proud of their heritage, often referring themselves as Basques first, then citizens of Spain. For marketers wanting to sell products to Spain, they must be aware that they must modify the marketing mix for residents in the Basque regions accordingly.

DEMOGRAPHIC SEGMENTATION

Dividing a group according to variables such as age, gender, marital status, income, occupation education, religion, and nationality is called **demographic segmentation**. Demographic segmentation is by far the most popular means of segmentation because they have traditionally been highly correlated to consumption patterns, meaning demographic variables have been very good at predicting consumer behaviour. Today, the predictive power of demographic data is not as effective as in the past. For example, the role of women has dramatically evolved in many industrialized countries in the last generation. In the past a women's age and marital status were strong predictors of whether she had borne children. Today, women are having their families later in life; a new mum can be anywhere from her 20s to her mid-40s and due to the wonders of in-vitro fertilization, even older. Though demographic segmentation is still widely used we should realize that as society change, demographic segmentation loses some of their predictive power. We now take a closer look at a few of these variables below.

GENDER

Forget for a moment that all people are created equal. Men and women need different products, and tend to differ in their approaches to meeting those needs. **Gender segmentation** entails dividing a market according to the gender of the customer, followed by a marketing offer consisting of a marketing-mix that is tailored to meet the unsatisfied needs of the targeted gender. Dividing the market according to gender is widely employed. Walk into a department store, and it becomes instantly clear which sections are targeted to women and which are targeted to men. It is equally dramatic for boy's and girl's clothing, few boys will be caught alive in pink, though girls are more opened minded about colours and clothing styles.

INCOME

Income segmentation entails dividing a market into classes according to the annual salary earned by consumers. Typically, these groups are divided into low, middle and high income groups. The marketing-mix targeted to those in the low income group will be different than those tailored to those who earn more. This can be seen in men's stores where we can buy clothing at Wal-Mart or ASDA; Sears, Target, Macy's or John Lewis; and Saks Fifth Avenue or Harrods, each a step up in the income ladder. In the retail industry, income segmentation is fraying a bit around the edges as well as some less well off people are also "spoiling" themselves by shopping a rung or two up the status ladder and some rather well off people will do some of their shopping at Wal-Mart or ASDA to save money in categories where they are content with less expensive goods.

LIFE-CYCLE SEGMENTATION

There are a number of marketers who believe that dividing markets according to their stage in their life-cycle provides better insight into predicting a consumer's behaviour versus traditional methods of demographic segmentation. The argument is persuasive. For the first time in recorded history, there are four different generations living on the earth at the same time. Colloquially known as Seniors, Baby-boomers, X-ers, and Nexters, their size, income, values and personal experiences greatly vary from each other. They therefore have different needs, and if they are large enough, will greatly influence which products are sold and when. We think this a new and particularly important new form of segmentation so we will spend a bit of time on it.

Beyond just the normal difference in age which takes place with every generation we believe that how they view the world is at times fundamentally different between the four generations. It is this worldview which marketers have got to get their heads around in order to successfully tailor their message to each generation. For example if you are trying to sell luxury with the seniors you may wish to stress the fact that the luxury good is the best buy because it lasts the longest and you will be able to pass it onto one of your grandchildren in your will. Boomers tend to be more interested with impressing people that they are successful and more wear their luxury on their selves, so talking about how respected the brand is will be more successful an approach. Xers tend to roll their eyes at the Boomers showing off so you point out how it is a private indulgence for them. One bugbear we have is that too many marketers are too youth oriented. For some products catering to this demographic is vital. For example podcasts seem to be reserved to the youth oriented world. That said, not every new web tool is the exclusive domain of teens. Blogs are one good example. Most marketers assume that bloggers and blog readers are young. However, according to a survey of more than 17,000 blog readers conducted by BlogAds, 61% of readers are 30 years of age and older, and 75% earn more than $45,000 a year. This study helps draw a picture of blog readers that is very different from what many had previously pictured.

We think that marketers are overly focused on the young and should spend much more time targeting the boomers. There are a lot of them, the number of older people is growing and they have the money. Marketers especially appreciate a segment which has money to spend and is willing, and in some cases even eager to spend it.

PSYCHOGRAPHIC SEGMENTATION

Psychographic segmentation entails dividing buyers into groups according to their lifestyles, personalities or personal values and attitudes. Psychographic segmentation is a technique that attempts to create a profile of how a particular group lives, what are their interests and what are their likes. This approach also allows the marketer to create groups that reaches across demographic and geographic segments. It is generally considered more powerful than traditional demographic segmentations like gender and income but has a major drawback in that it is harder to get data on where people's "heads are at". Things like magazines they subscribe to, *Condé Nast* suggest a sophisticated traveller or at least a wanabee, where they live or where they take their holidays are markers but it is still an imprecise science identifying segments by psychographics, though a particularly powerful one when you can identify people this way.

LIFESTYLE

Dividing buyers according to lifestyle reveals the daily activities a particular group engages in. How the segment lives will affect the types of products they consume. For example, those that are savvy with technology will often be the first to purchase the latest software, or hardware. An interesting example of a lifestyle grouping is the billion-dollar worldwide urban lifestyle market. It is arguably the top aspirational luxury lifestyle of the youth market. The same market that has been burning an increasing sum of money on items like Phat Farm polo T-shirts that cost $75 or more. Centred around urban music stars and their lifestyles, the urban market's potential was first discovered by Russell Simmons' rap group Run DMC in 1986 with their song "My Adidas". After its release, the shoe quickly became a symbol of 1980s rap culture. More recently, even McDonald's has jumped in with the introduction of its "I'm Lovin' It" slogan. It commissioned local urban market specialists across North America to give street cred to the slogan prior to the official launch. Buzz marketing is particularly useful in this marketplace. Here are some key pointers from an article Karl and his former student, Laura Mingail wrote about reaching urban markets:

> **Be exclusive** Like the urban lifestyle that so many pre-teens, teenagers and even young adults want a part of, successful buzz targeting this lucrative segment should be

perceived as privileged information. Once something becomes common knowledge, it loses its buzz-worthiness, just as an urban brand is cool until it becomes commercial. Those who have the privilege of hearing buzz feel like they belong to an elite group. So spread the buzz only to tastemakers and those next in line down the hierarchy of cool. The rest will be sure to catch on as they actively seek out trends and don't wait for trends to come to them.

Be original If you try to imitate other successful buzz tactics, you risk having your brand perceived as the "follower" as opposed to the "cool brand". A unique brand requires unique buzz. Get your chief designer and their team involved; he or she absolutely understands the soul of the brand and intuitively understands how to present it in a way that resonates.

Stay true to your brand Don't be a sell-out. For example, if your brand is firmly established as a family brand or a commercial teen brand, it may be hard to create true street credibility. The buzz could even backfire by positioning your brand as one that's trying too hard to be cool. Or it could confuse your existing customers, causing them to look elsewhere.

Know where that buzz comes from The medium is the message when it comes to ad placement, and the same rule applies here. Some may argue that as long as the message spreads, you're doing your job. Not true. Buzz is created by word of mouth, which has a strong effect on shaping first impressions of your brand. You'll have a hard time conveying the message that your brand is "cool" if the person passing on the message isn't cool at all or if the buzz is seen as an obvious corporate ploy. Just as there are tastemakers there are also taste-killers.

Having your product or service perceived as commercial will significantly deter urban-oriented customers. As most corporations are considered commercial, the perception of the origin of the buzz is key. Here, you have two options: Begin by giving street cred to your company, or distance yourself as much as possible from the buzz tactics. The former long-term strategy has proven to be the profitable choice of brands like Phat Farm and Rocawear, founded by hip-hop moguls Russell Simmons and rapper Jay-Z. If you're just looking to give street cred to one of your brands, the latter tactic is recommended.

Act locally People are becoming increasingly aware of discrete marketing ploys. You cannot always rely on celebrities to act as believable tastemakers if they're seen as being in it for the money. Such celebrities don't create authentic buzz they simply pass along a firm's message. Local buzz and urban marketing experts know which local tastemakers to target depending on your strategy, and how local urban markets will react to different buzz tactics. If you want to do it on your own, you've got to become a credible part of the market, and start building extensive databases.

PERSONALITY

Segmenting a market according to personality traits such as spontaneity, sophistication and the ever elusive "cool", is another type of psychographic segmentation. Once a set of personality traits have been identified, the marketer crafts a promotional campaign associating their product to those traits.

VALUES AND ATTITUDES

The fourth type of psychographic segmentation is to divide a market according to values and attitudes. Happiness, reason, virtue, honour, individualism, free will and love are some examples of values whereas good governance, and ethical behaviour are examples of attitudes. Dividing a market according to values and attitudes enables the marketer to craft a promotional campaign that associates their brand to those held by a particular group. For example, as consumers become more aware of how their purchasing habits direct world trade, many are choosing to buy products that are certified as fair-trade, a seal that assures the buyer the supplier of the commodity was paid the market price.

BEHAVIOURAL SEGMENTATION

In **behavioural segmentation**, the marketer divides buyers into groups based on the benefit sought, their loyalty to the brand, their readiness to buy, the product's usage rate, the product's end use and the customer's attitude toward the product.

BENEFIT SOUGHT

As we have mentioned in chapter three, a product is a complex bundle of benefits. Creating segments according to the benefits they receive will allow the firm to better understand buyer motivation. Knowing what motivates buyers aids the marketer in crafting their promotional campaign.

BRAND LOYALTY

Dividing a market according to brand loyalty reveals the response rates of the marketing-mix. Typically, buyers are divided into the following four categories:

Platinum Customers who always buy the brand.
Gold Customers who will buy the brand most of the time, occasionally choose another.
Silver Customers who are indifferent to all brands in the category.
Bronze Customers who have no loyalty to the brand whatsoever.

Marketers should concentrate their marketing efforts on promoting customers from silver to gold, gold to platinum and ensuring their platinum customers never flee. Those that are in the bronze category should be ignored because they will never demonstrate loyalty to the brand irrespective of the marketing-mix.

READINESS TO BUY

This process entails dividing people according to which stage of the buying process they reside within. The buying process consists of six stages: First a consumer is *unaware* of a product's benefits. Second, after being exposed to a promotional campaign, they become *somewhat aware*. Following repeated exposure, they become *informed*. The more informed they become the more *interested* they become in the product. This in turn increases their *desire* to own the product, which finally translates into an *intention to buy*. The stage a product exists within the buying process affects the type of promotional campaign that is implemented.

USAGE RATE

Markets can also be segmented according to rate of usage. Typically marketers divide the market into heavy, medium and light users. Heavy users, generally speaking, are the smallest group a marketer serves, but they are the most profitable. Promoting a small percentage of medium users into heavy users will dramatically affect the bottom line. It is the commonly quoted 80/20 rule, where 80% of your sales come from 20% of your customers, a rule which holds in an amazing number of markets.

PRODUCT END USE

Another method of segmenting a market is to identify the current status of the consumer. Marketers normally group customers into the following categories: regular users, first-time users, former users, competitive users, and non-users. Regular users are the most valuable and contribute the most to profit. The challenge with first-time users is to make it such a positive experience that they will be converted to become regular users. Former users are of considerable interest. A starting place is to ask why did they leave? There are good reasons and poor reasons. A good reason might be that your product is no longer relevant, they have moved to a different city or have retired, a poor reason is that you dropped the ball on the customer service front. Poor reasons are ones you should try to solve and win back their business. Users of your competitors' product are of great interest. After your own users they are a critical target. The great advantage is that they are already users of your product's category and believe that it is relevant to their lives; what you must do is figure out why they buy from your competitor and not you. What is it that Lexus can do to win over drivers from BMW and Mercedes? Non-users are harder work.

Here the marketer must do missionary work, trying to convert the non-user to become a believer in the product category. Fizzy water companies have done an excellent job in the last decade converting many Americans to drinking bottled water, their missionary work has paid off for them but also for Coke and Pepsi who also now sell water in big numbers in North America. A good thing in a time of great concern about obesity which has impacted on sales of soft drinks negatively and sales of water positively. These days Coke machines not only offer Coke but also water and juices as healthy alternatives.

CONSUMER ATTITUDES

Consumer attitudes toward the product can also be used to segment a market. Consumers can hold a fanatic, positive, indifferent, negative or hostile attitude toward the product. Knowing what the customer thinks about the product, greatly aids in crafting the promotional message.

OCCASIONS

Finally, grouping buyers according to the occasions for when a product is purchased or consumed is another means of dividing a market to learn more about a consumer's behaviour. With this knowledge, a marketer can modify the marketing mix to encourage a change in consumption patterns. An interesting example is the marketing done by DeBeers of South Africa about diamonds. A number of years ago they ran ads offering the advice that a man should spend 2 months salary when buying an engagement ring for his beloved. Men, not knowing better, accepted this advice from a truly biased source and this has become widely accepted in the US. A more recent campaign makes the point that if your wife stuck around with you for 25 years the least you can do is buy her another diamond ring. Again, men, not knowing better accepted this advice from a well and truly biased source. Their latest campaign in Japan is targeted at getting single women to realize that they can buy a nice diamond ring on their own, they don't need a man and use a attractive, single Japanese female movie star as the their spokeswoman. In each case they are trying and generally succeeding in expanding sales by widening the number of occasions that you might buy a diamond ring.

FINAL THOUGHTS ON SEGMENTATION

Marketers rarely use only one segmentation method. Each methodology we have discussed has certain advantages and disadvantages. By using a combination of approaches, the marketer gains insight on the different dimensions of their customers. **Oversegmentation** can occur, which is when a marketer unnecessarily segments the market. Just because consumers express the desire to have products more closely tailored to fit their needs, that doesn't mean they won't purchase the product altogether, the key principle to keep in mind as they only adjust the levers of the marketing mix upward if it will result in more revenue than the cost incurred.

TARGETING THE MARKET

Choosing your **target market** is the process of evaluating each segment's attractiveness and choosing which one or ones to go after. Which markets to enter depends on the corporate strategy and the company's resources. One of the hardest things to do for many marketers is to choose their target segments and stick with them, ignoring other segments. Learning to say "no" is very hard but is critical because any firm, even the largest, have only limited resources.

EVALUATING MARKET SEGMENTS

When evaluating to which segments to offer a product, a firm considers three factors: the size and growth opportunities, the existing industrial structure and the company's objectives and capabilities. The company collects and analyses data on each segment, calculating the current sales, projected growth rates and expected profit levels. Those that meet the company's size and growth requirements are then placed under closer scrutiny. At this stage, the investigator analyses the capabilities of the competition, the buying power of suppliers, the buying power of buyers, the availability of substitutes. In other words, a segment must undergo a Porter Analysis.

Lastly, if a segment is of the right size and growth potential, as well as having a favourable industrial structure, the company must consider their corporate objectives and capabilities. If entering the segment is counter to the stated objectives of the firm, or if the firm does not have the resources, skills or contacts to properly service the segment, they should reject the entry proposition. To win in a segment, a firm must offer superior value over the existing alternatives.

SELECTING TARGET MARKET SEGMENTS

Once the firm decides which segment or segments to serve, they have five entry strategies: single-segment concentration, selective specialization, product specialization, market specialization and full-market coverage

SINGLE-SEGMENT CONCENTRATION

In this strategy, the vendor decides to target only one segment, and concentrate all their efforts into capturing a leadership position. With a leadership position, the firm can maximize the economies of scale, control the distribution channels and develop a loyal customer base. They can also be seen as "the" supplier in a particular segment, that is their focus, that is what they are truly world class at.

SELECTIVE SPECIALIZATION

This strategy entails entering more than one segment. By entering a number of attractive segments, the firm spreads their operating risk, and their investments along a number of potentially profitable ventures. A key question to ask yourself is to identify if any synergies exist between the segments you operate within. In other words, does offering a product in one segment contribute to the success of another product in another?

PRODUCT SPECIALIZATION

This is a strategy employed by manufacturers with a product that can be tailored to meet the needs of different segments. For example, some high-tech software products like People Soft or SAP go after just one type of product (Enterprise Software in SAP's case) but tailor it a wide variety of segments.

MARKET SPECIALIZATION

With a market specialization strategy a firm is attempting to lever their good standing with a profitable segment by offering them more products to fulfil other unmet needs. Grocery stores are increasingly offering their customers more products other than foods and consumer durables; clothing, furniture and even financial services are offered to customers. Wal-Mart is now one of the largest food retailers in the US; one analyst reported that "it sells 19% of all grocery-store food in the United States, and it handles 16% of all pharmacy-drug sales in the United States, and plans to increase that share to 25% by 2008, which would make it the largest pharmacy in America".

FULL MARKET COVERAGE

As the name suggests, full market coverage is a strategy where the vendor serves every segment available. Vendors with a full product-line are capable of undertaking a full-market coverage strategy. The vendor can choose to pursue an *undifferentiated* approach or a *differentiated* approach. Employing an undifferentiated approach entails treating different segments as one market. In other words, the vendor tailors the marketing-mix to appeal to needs held in common between all segments. An undifferentiated approach is the polar opposite of a differentiated approach. This strategy entails designing a different product to each segment. Automobile manu-facturers and increasingly, airline companies are employing a differentiated full-market coverage strategy.

POSITIONING

We now turn to positioning a product. As we have repeatedly stated, understanding customer needs and delivering more value than other products are the keys to winning and keeping customers. But in every segment there can only be one leader. That is, unless the customer recognizes distinctions exist between products. These distinctions can be drawn by highlighting differences in quality, price, performance and other things relevant to the customer. There can be multiple leaders in a single market. Take the automobile industry for example. Though every manufacturer builds cars, a BMW 750 is seen as a different car than a Honda Civic. Consumers recognize these differences because vendors practice **product positioning**. Product positioning entails **differentiating** a product from competitors by highlighting important attributes and benefits.

CHOOSING A POSITIONING STRATEGY

One way to accomplish this is to create advertising that draws a mental map of the product's benefits in contrast to a competitor's offering. By contrasting a product's key features and benefits against the shortcomings of the competition, the customer will create a mental map in their mind differentiating the advertised product from the competition.

In today's world, people in consumerist societies are bombarded with thousands of images each and every day. In order to process all of this information, studies have shown that people form **product ladders** in their minds. Product ladders are a mental ranking system, except, once a product has been accepted as the best in its category, it is very difficult for other products to displace it. For example, many people will be able to tell you who is the current captain of England's football team. But can you recall the name of the player David Beckham replaced? Not so easy is it?

For products that failed to climb up to the highest step, the marketer has four options. The first is to strengthen their current position. Sony's VAIO laptops are more expensive than comparable models. However, their laptops have long battery lives and one version of the product weighs less than 2kg, lending the company to position their laptop as the preferred choice for users who are constantly moving and place convenience as their top priority.

A second strategy is to grab an unoccupied position. Though a number of companies were involved in the business of professional wrestling, the WWE were the first to brand their product as sports entertainment. By admitting their matches are staged, the rules are malleable and are bent in favour of the cast of colourful personalities, the WWE turned the sport of professional wrestling into a billion dollar soap opera.

A third approach is to reposition. Repositioning requires a large investment if the product has been heavily advertised in the past. As oil supplies dwindle worldwide, Shell Oil has been quietly repositioning itself as an energy supplier that offers a wide range of renewable and non-renewable energy sources. In 2005 the Hawaii Tourism Board sought to reposition Hawaii in the mind of its second most important market, Japanese tourists. In the past it had used Hawaii Sumo wrestlers in their ads in Japan. In 2005 they launched ads using a hot young ukulele player, Jake Shimabukuro, to present a different positioning of Hawaii in Japanese minds. Beyond the cool of Jake they also used a new tag line, "The islands of Aloha". First was to signal to Japanese who tend to stay the Waikiki beach when they are in Hawaii and tend to think of Waikiki as being Hawaii, by highlighting the fact that 8 major islands make up the chain of Hawaii of islands. Thus they were suggesting that there was a lot more to explore in Hawaii than just the urban beach of Waikiki. Insiders say the repositioning has been quite successful in getting the Japanese to experience the many charms of the Hawaiian Islands.

Finally, creating an exclusive club is a strategy to position a product. Accountancy firms are often referred to as the Big Five. While there are tens of thousands of accountancy firms, whenever someone in the business world hears the words "Big Five", most immediately recall the names of all five firms. It's a neat party trick to out the accountant.

Positioning a product in the mind of a consumer is very controversial. Some have accused the practice as being a form of brainwashing. Perhaps we shouldn't be surprised that the idea of crafting a message specifically to position a product in the mind of a consumer was pioneered by advertising executives, but the fact is that people will always position products spatially in their minds if they can perceive a difference exists. The marketer exists to make an economic profit by providing a product that satisfies needs and wants. Marketers therefore will never leave their product positioning to chance. They will design their communications strategy to ensure people realize differences exist to give their product the greatest advantage in their target markets.

A less controversial approach would be to position the firm, not the product, as either a product leader, operationally excellent, or customer-responsive. It has been observed that a firm cannot excel in all three categories. Being a product leader means the firm must continually advance the technological frontier. This requires large investments in R&D, which need to be recouped later on, making it very difficult for a firm to be a product leader and the lowest cost producer. What's more, firms that are customer-responsive try to tailor their product offering to exactly match the customer's wants. The more customized the product, the higher the cost of production, which once again makes it very difficult for a firm to be operationally efficient and customer responsive.

As such, firms that are seeking to position themselves must follow the following four rules:

1   Develop a leadership position in one of the three positions.
2   Preserve a satisfactory level of performance in the other categories.
3   Continue to improve on the leadership position the firm occupies.
4   Improve on the other two positions to keep aligned with innovating competitors.

IDENTIFY POSSIBLE COMPETITIVE ADVANTAGES

After identifying which points of contact a firm contains a source of competitive advantage, it must decide which contact points to select and which features to promote as a means of **differentiating** their product from others. Differentiation is the process of adding a set of meaningful and valued differences distinguishing the company's product offering from other substitutes.

One approach suggests the firm promotes only one benefit. By offering a consumer a **unique selling proposition** vendors can develop one consistent positioning message enabling buyers to quickly associate the product with the promoted feature. Though single-benefit positioning is a cost-effective positioning strategy, eventually, some competitor, new innovation, or change in consumer preferences threatens a firm's leadership position.

Since a firm's leadership position is eventually threatened by competition, innovation or changes in consumer preferences, it stands to reason promoting more than one benefit hedges against these potential treats. Exactly how many benefits to promote cannot be addressed directly because the issue largely depends on the type of product being offered. Generally speaking a product should be positioned according to these four rules:

1   Never under-position. Under-positioning occurs when customers cannot readily identify the brand or the brand's features. The product must stand out in the mind of the consumer.
2   Never over-position. Over-positioning occurs when the brand is promoted too narrowly. Volvo is still regarded as a car manufacturer that makes safe, reliable and durable automobiles. Few realize that Volvo also offers a critically acclaimed sports car.
3   Never over-promote. Highlighting every possible benefit, or changing the brand's positioning frequently will confuse buyers.
4   Never over-promise. Over-promising usually works for politicians, but history has shown consumer backlash is swift against firms that make dubious claims about their product's features, quality or value.

A customer's overall impression of a company is formed through their experience with the firm's product, service, people, channels of distribution and product image. These five points of contact provide a firm with the opportunity to develop competitive advantages over their competitors, thus allowing the firm to differentiate themselves. A word of caution: a firm *must* offer and *must* deliver superior value and quality on those dimensions on which they differentiate themselves because customers constantly incorporate past experience into their decision making processes. The actual experience of dealing with all too many firms falls short of their marketing hype. The result is a turned off customer. Research suggests that a very dissatisfied customer will be much more active in noising their unhappiness to other potential customers than very happy customers. Auditing the actual customer experience to see how it measures is something an increasing number of firms are doing. Let's now take a closer look at the five points of contact that can be a possible source of competitive advantage.

PRODUCT DIFFERENTIATION

The actual product provides a great degree of latitude when it comes to differentiation. The manufacturer can adjust the form of the product by modifying the shape, size or structure of the product to differentiate it from other products. A second source of product differentiation is to add (or remove) additional features to the product. What an increasing number of firms find is that after several years of adding features they do well by introducing a slimmed down basic product which appeals those with less complex needs and to budget conscious consumers. Telephone companies are finding this, as they add Call Waiting, Call Answer, Caller ID, etc., that there exists a substantial market which only wants basic phone service, be it landline or cellular. A third would be to attain a consistent level of quality. Fast food is by no means the healthiest of meals. McDonald's strategy is to consistently deliver low priced, quality food. A key part of their value proposition is that it will be very predictable what you will get. Pre-MacDonald's when you travelled you never were sure what surprises, unpleasant or perhaps pleasant, the local "greasy spoon" held in store. When you see a MacDonald's in Peoria, Illinois, Pretoria, South Africa or Perth, Australia you know that it will be a familiar menu, remind you of home, regardless of where you are from and will please the children.

A fourth source of differentiation is to create a product with high durability. A fifth is creating a product that is reliable over the product's life. In case the vendor focuses on the cost of ownership, that is costs not only of buying the product, called Capital expenditure (CAPEX) but also installing (IMPEX) and operating (OPEX) it. In the case of the infrastructure of cell stations necessary to run a national cellphone network, the cost of maintenance or operating it may be equal to the cost of buying it over a ten-year period. To ignore the cost of operating the system would obviously be a poor away of analysing the true cost of the project.

A sixth is to offer a product that is easy to repair. One of the main attractions of the original VW Beetle was that general repairs did not require a mechanic. Often a garden hose and duct tape sufficed. Finally, changing the design and style of the product differentiates the product from the competition. Fashion items, such as *haute couture* clothing or high-end athletic shoes often have a yearly or even seasonal life to them. One would not want to be seen in last year's Dior smock!

SERVICE DIFFERENTIATION

In segments such as commodity markets where consumers do not easily recognize differences between products, offering specialized services translates into a competitive advantage, and thus differentiates one firm from another. Simplifying the ordering process or offering delivery services are two such methods. Air Canada has simplified the buying process for many of their customers by reducing from hundreds of potential fares for a flight to just 5, they have also moved online and eliminated the need for paper tickets in the vast majority of cases. Providing installation and maintenance expertise are another two. Many high-tech firms will have maintenance personal located at their key customer's site in order to cut travel time to zero, resulting in great service and reduced downtime for their customer. Customer training programs and providing after-sales service also leaves a positive impression in the customer's mind.

PERSONNEL DIFFERENTIATION

Companies can differentiate themselves by hiring highly trained and knowledgeable staff. Their employees' overall competence, courtesy, reliability, responsiveness, communication skills and their trustworthiness all factor in the differentiation process. Part of IBM's advertising campaign is to feature some members of a product team. The aim is to illustrate that IBM is staffed by highly competent and dedicated employees, which in turn puts a human face to an organization that has long been known only as Big Blue.

CHANNEL DIFFERENTIATION

Practising channel differentiation is another source of competitive advantage. Developing the expertise to manage a large distribution network efficiently requires considerable investment and expertise that is difficult to replicate. Firms that develop a competitive advantage through their channels to market translate into an expectation by the consumer that they can depend on the firm to have their products available wherever the consumer currently resides. Learjet, which makes business jets for busy executives, offers outstanding parts service in remote areas of the world, speeding the time of recovery on the rare occasion your jet breaks down, a problem we would like to have to worry about!

IMAGE DIFFERENTIATION

Firms that practice image differentiation distance their product from the competition by cultivating distinct identities for their brand. One way to craft a distinct identity is to create a symbol that represents the brand. The image of the self-confident, independent minded Marlboro Man is heralded as the reason why Philip Morris' Marlboro cigarettes were so successful. Developing catchy slogans, sponsoring public events also adds to image development. But a word of caution when it comes to image differentiation; fantasy can turn to a nightmare quickly. Just as the Marlboro Man was successful marketing the cigarette brand with his name, shortly after his death, due to lung cancer no less, Phillip Morris and other tobacco companies are paying billions to various levels of government because they failed to properly warn users about the risks of smoking.

SELECTING A POSITIONING STRATEGY

Once the firm identifies its competitive advantages over its competitors, it must select which one or ones to promote in order to differentiate their product from their competitors. All else constant, a consumer chooses the product that provides the greatest value. Therefore, positioning a product on the features and benefits that maximizes customer value means the product stands the best chance of succeeding in the marketplace. Marketers define the full positioning of a product as a **value proposition**. Figure 7.1 is a picture of a model developed by marketing guru Philip Kotler illustrating five successful value propositions and four unsuccessful ones. For the sake of brevity, we will only discuss successful ones.

MORE FOR MORE

This strategy entails offering the highest quality product at the highest price. This strategy is employed by vendors that position their product as being one that has high quality and provides the buyer high prestige. Haagen Daaz ice cream, Starbucks coffee, Rolex watches are but some examples of products that promise buyers more benefits for more money.

The More-for-More strategy can leave a product vulnerable to competition. If the price differential between the product and the competition is sufficiently larger than the difference in quality offered, eventually consumers choose the firm that offers a value proposition of more benefits for the same price. This means that firms in this market space must be constantly innovating to keep their brand ahead of competition.

MORE FOR THE SAME

Offering more benefits for the same price is a competition-killer. Once customers recognize they receive more value at the same cost, they choose the product that offers the highest value. Due to the dramatic effects the more for the same strategy can produce, companies protect their products by patenting critical processes or parts, creating a brand name, or employ other defensive strategies

Figure 7.1 Value Proposition Matrix

		More	The same	Less
Price	More	More for more	More for the same	More for less
	The same	Unsuccessful strategy	Unsuccessful strategy	The same for less
	Less	Unsuccessful strategy	Unsuccessful strategy	Less for much less

to reduce the erosion in market share if a competitor introduces a product that offers more for the same.

MORE FOR LESS

Positioning a product to offer more benefits at a price lower than the competition is another winning strategy. Firms can offer more for less when they discover a new breakthrough that radically changes the standard business model. Dell Computers was one such company. The computer industry is very competitive and because of the ubiquity of computers, it has many of the characteristics of a commodity market. Because margins are extremely thin, cost-savings have a dramatic effect on the bottom line.

Dell was one of the first companies to pioneer the idea of **mass-customization**, where the manufacturer offers a basic skeleton and the customer selects the parts. Customers could order their custom-made computer either on the Internet or on the telephone, the entire process taking a few minutes. Furthermore, on the cost side of the business, Dell was one of the first companies to use **just-in-time** (JIT) delivery systems. With JIT, they never held a component in inventory for longer than a week. Low inventory costs enabled Dell to have lower prices and offer customers a product that provides high value.

Unfortunately a more for less strategy cannot be sustained in the long-term. Competitors adapt their business models to match or better the offered benefits. Prices will fall because consumers in the long-term have grown accustomed to a lower price for the product.

SAME FOR LESS

This strategy is used if the firm wants to build market share. Positioning a product that offers the same benefits for a reduced price is one of the oldest strategies in business. In the IBM compatible mainframe marketplace there are two competitors, IBM and Fujitsu. Part of Fujitsu's offer is that they are just as good as IBM, you can roll out your IBM mainframe and roll in the Fujitsu equivalent and your software will run just the same, but Fujitsu is considerably less expensive. If the offering can be sustained, eventually, it will force the competition to exit the market. There is perhaps no industry other than the retailing industry that has been so radically affected by firms employing the same for less strategy. Firms such as Carrefour, Wal-Mart and other big box stores, build airplane hangar sized stores, filling the shelves with nearly every consumer product imaginable at prices that no other smaller sized competitor can match for sustained periods of time. It is no wonder why these big-box stores are called **category killers**.

LESS FOR MUCH LESS

This strategy is similar to the strategy in that the vendor is attempting to undercut its rivals. However the firm cannot match the benefits offered to the customer, so the vendor therefore reduces the price to a level low enough to entice consumers to switch. No one can resist a deal, it's just a matter of finding the right price. Many customers are perfectly happy to have a "bare bones" product for much cheaper, they just don't need the functionality that others do. Students often find themselves in this segment.

COMMUNICATING THE POSITIONING

Once the positioning of the product has been established, the firm must develop a positioning statement which they will centre their promotion campaign around. A typical positioning statement takes the form:

> To (name of target market) who are seeking (list the unsatisfied need) or wants our (product name) is (product type) that (list the point or points of differentiation).

Here is an opportunity where we can engage in an act of shameless self-promotion. With rare exceptions, academic textbooks cost far too much, have far too much useless information. It is for these reasons we decided to write this book. Though we did not write a positioning statement, had we done so, it would read:

> To all students and practitioners tired of contributing to the retirement plans of publishers abusing their market power by offering expensive

and voluminous textbooks, our textbook, *Marketing: The Basics*, is the only book that gives you the vital information you need to excel in any marketing related activity without the need to donate your kidney to fund your educational need.

We worked very hard to ensure you keep all your vital organs where they belong.

FINAL THOUGHTS ON POSITIONING

To finish up on this important topic we will suggest five important dimensions to test your firm's positioning against:

Differentiation occurs along 5 dimensions:

1   Importance – the difference delivers a highly valued benefit that members of your target market actually care about. This is the acid test of the marketplace and we put it first because it is the most important.

2   Distinctive – the difference is noticeable and believable with the target segment. They have got to believe that you are different!

3   Superior – no other product matches the quality of your product on the key dimensions, your product simply delivers better on these benefits than the competition.

4   Unique – the benefit cannot be copied easily, that is you have something which can be used successfully for a number of years and not quickly imitated by your competitors, bringing you back down to an even playing field, there is little profit here.

5   Affordable – the benefit is affordable to the buyer and not perceived as overpriced.

6   Profitable – it makes economic sense to provide the benefit. If you are not going to make money why bother, of course in the early days of a product you don't expect to be immediately profitable. Sometimes the product is good over the longer term, but some products just never get there. Learn to have the discipline to axe them early rather than later in the process. This takes great discipline and considerable market insight, but is one of the signs of a great marketer.

BRANDS AND EXPERIENCE

Throughout this book we have talked about brands. In this section we define what a brand is and suggest some ways brands can be effectively used. The American Marketing Association defines a brand as "a name, term, sign, symbol, or design, or a combination of them, intended to identify the goods, or services of one seller or group of sellers and to differentiate them from those of competitors". A brand then, is a product or service that adds dimensions that differentiate it, in some way relevant for the customer, from other products designed to satisfy the same name. The differences may be functional, rational or tangible, that is related to the product performance of the brand. They may also be symbolic, emotional or intangible, that is related to what the brand represents in the mind of the consumer.

Branding is hardly a new thing. Marketing historians have traced back the first brands to Ancient Greece. One of the key industries in that day was the pottery industry. The industry catered almost exclusively to consumer demand. The entrepreneurs that catered to this nascent consumer market were mostly craftsmen who quickly responded to economic incentives and pressures. Modern archaeologists have traced different pots to their respective makers and workshops by grouping the designs the potter used. Strong evidence shows that by the 6th century BCE, potters mostly from Corinth, were producing pots targeted to specific markets stretching from Spain to the Black Sea. Athenian potters, locked out of the niche markets by more responsive Corinthian competitors, appear to have chosen a mass-market approach, producing vessels of a lesser artistic quality destined for foreign markets. Eventually they realized that in markets that offered consumers a variety of choices, a differentiation strategy was needed to separate their product from other competitors. Branding was born.

As early as the 7th century BCE the potters of Euboea began to label their work. This practice spread to Athens and Corinth in the following century. Sophilos appears to be the first Athenian potter to identify his own work; around the top of his vases he sometimes etched images of the Gods of Athens. Another craftsman, Euthymides, bragged on one of his creations that his vase was of a higher quality than those of Euphronios, the first example we have found of "slagging off" a competitor! The potter's signature, suggests both a pride in his product and a desire to attract future orders.

Once branding became prevalent, advertising claims soon followed. A motto on a cup imported to Italy from Rhodes may be the first recorded commercial advertisement. It read, "Nestor had a most drink-worthy cup, but whoever drinks of mine will straightaway be smitten with the desire of fair-crowned Aphrodite". Who can resist the desires of the Goddess of Love? Even in Ancient Greece, sex sells.

Brands have evolved to be something much more important and complex. Brands identify the source of a product and allow customers, whether consumer or organizations, to value the product differently because of the source. Customers learn about brands by past experience with the product. They learn to value some brands more than others. At the heart of this is ability of brands to simplify our buying in a hectic and time starved world and reduce risk by the promise of quality that a brand delivers. When we buy a Ralph Lauren polo shirt we realize that we could spend less money but the polo horse on the shirt means that we bought a good quality shirt, it reduces our risk of buying. It also makes our search for that new shirt that much easier, we don't have to go from shop to shop endlessly comparing goods to find one that we will feel comfortable with. It also may give us "street cred" or social status among other people. These are three of the key advantages of brands to the customer.

Where do brands apply? In virtually every category. It is possible to brand a physical good, a service (British Airways, Bank of Tokyo) a store (Nike, Holt Renfrew), a person (John Grisham, Philip Kotler) a place (the Lake District, Niagara Falls) an organization or an idea (British Automobile Association, UNICEF).

Brands can be both repositioned and rejuvenated. We gave an example of repositioning a few pages ago with the example of the repositioning of Hawaii in the Japanese market. Rejuvenating a brand can be critical to breathing life back in a brand which may have become burnished over time. A recent good example of this is the way the hot selling Razor Cellphone has added gleam to Motorola's reputation for innovative and beautifully designed products. The Razor, in case you have not seen one, is a super thin, or at least by previous standards super thin, cellphone. The first internal estimates of sales were 500,000. Take off was so rapid that soon over 1 million were quickly sold. The success of the Razor was quickly followed up by a raft of follow on products. The Razor and its' descendants caused a considerable buzz and added renewed lustre to Motorola's brand reputation for innovation and design.

SUMMARY

- The marketing mix is designed specifically to position a product in the minds of the target market.
- Segmentation methods are used to select the target market.
- A winning positioning strategy places the product at the top of a customer's product ladder.
- Brands offer a complex set of unique benefits that offer many potential sources of competitive advantage.

CRITICAL QUESTIONS

1   List and discuss the various methods of segmenting a market.
2   Explain how companies position their products in the mind of consumers. What role does each element of the marketing mix play?
3   What is a unique selling proposition? Should a company position a product solely on a unique selling proposition or more?
4   Discuss the various position strategies available to a marketer. What are the advantages of each? What could an incumbent do to counter these strategies?
5   Why is differentiation so important? List and describe the five dimensions a marketer can use to differentiate a product.

SUGGESTIONS FOR FURTHER READING

Al Ries and Jack Trout, *Positioning: The Battle for Your Mind*, Toronto: McGraw-Hill, 2000.

A revised and updated version of the classic book which really launched the idea of positioning. Written by a couple of New York advertising guys it is a light but insightful read.

Ken Dychtwald, *Age Power: How the 21st Century Will Be Ruled by the New Old*, New York, Tarcher Paper, 2002.

One of the most important of new ways of segmenting is by demographics; this book is an excellent way of introducing yourself to the subject.

Valarie Zeithaml, Roland Rust, and Katherine Lemon, *Driving Customer Equity*, New York, The Free Press, 2000.

A great book that outlines the important idea of segmenting your customers by profitability.

GLOSSARY

Behavioural segmentation   Dividing a market into groups based on the benefit sought.

Category killers   Vendors that sell so much and so many different products they eliminate niche players that reside within traditional product boundaries.

Differentiating   A strategy a seller uses to distance their product from another by emphasizing its unique features, benefits or qualities.

Demographic segmentation   Dividing a target market on the basis of social identifiers, such as age, family size, income, gender, education, occupation, religion, social class etc.

Gender segmentation   Dividing a market according to gender.

Geographic segmentation   Dividing a market into smaller geographical units.

Income segmentation   Dividing a market according to income levels.

Just-in-time delivery   A supply chain concept whereby goods arrive at a place only when they are required.

Life-cycle segmentation   Dividing a market into different stages of life.

Market segmentation   Dividing a heterogeneous market into smaller groups of similar characteristics.

Mass-customization   An offering where the customer can tailor a generic product to their tastes.

Oversegmentation   Dividing a market into groups that are unprofitable to serve.

Product ladders   A mental ranking system a consumer employs to sort products in a particular category.

Product positioning   Deliberately crafting a marketing mix separating the product from competitors.

Psychographic segmentation   Dividing a market into different groups based on attitudes, personal values, lifestyles or personalities.

Target market   The market the producer decides to market their product to.

Unique selling proposition   Differentiating a product based on benefit.

Value proposition   The offer a producer makes to a customer.

8

MARKET RESEARCH

Seeking Deep Insight into the
Customer's World and Mind

In the last chapter we discussed how marketers use Segmentation,
Targeting and Positioning (STP) to position their product. Underlying
the STP process are hundreds of hours dedicated to data collection
and analysis. This information is then used to gain a better insight
into the customer's mind and the world in which they live.
Questions about the industry structure, the competition, economic
trends, new advances in research and technology shifts in consumer
behaviour all fall under the rubric of **market research**. This chapter
focuses on two main areas, first we look at the decision making
process a consumer goes through, we then investigate the different
methods marketers use to collect market research.

INTRODUCTION TO CONSUMER BEHAVIOUR

In the previous chapters we talked about how marketers are responsible for communicating to the consumer the benefits of the
product, and point out how their product differs from their
competitors. Once the marketer has done so, it is the customer's
turn to respond. But how does the customer make a decision? The
stimulus-response model illustrated in Figure 8.1 demonstrates
how the process unfolds. Marketing and other stimuli from a
buyer's environment enters into a buyer's mind. Once in the mind,

which is essentially a **black box**, a number of transformations occur resulting in a response.

Once a buyer absorbs information sent by the marketer, the **buyer decision process** begins. In general the buyer decision process consists of five steps. The first is **need recognition**. The buyer recognizes a need exists. Then the buyer engages in an **information search**. At this stage, the buyer seeks information that enables them to make an informed decision. They rely on their own memory, the advice of friends, experts and advertising. The third stage is called the **evaluation of alternatives** stage. Here the customer weighs the possible pros and cons between available choices. The type of marketing mix, the buyer's purchasing habits and their desire for variety are all taken into consideration before the fourth stage or **purchase decision** begins. Finally, how the customer reacts to their purchase is captured in their **post-purchase behaviour** or **buyer's remorse**. The larger the gap between their expectations and the product's **perceived performance**, the greater the level of disappointment.

The buyer-stimulus model is useful to understand some but not all buying decisions. For example, think about how you might buy a can of Coke. If you are a Coke fan, you may well skip almost all the steps of this model. You may well find yourself buying a Coke at a class break without even thinking that you are thirsty but you do it out of habit or your body at some subconscious level lets you know

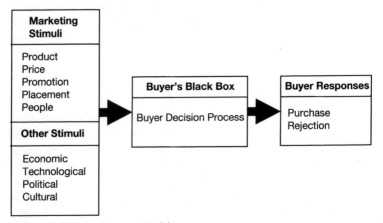

Figure 8.1 Stimulus-Response Model

you are thirsty. As long as there's a Coke available, you're probably going to skip the information search stage, since you decided in the past, that Coke satisfies your need. Now if you find yourself in front of a vending machine without Coke available, then you may have to think about what to buy or ignore your craving completely. As far as post-purchase behaviour or **buyer's remorse** is concerned, short of finding a mouse in the can, you will rarely if ever, think about your purchase of a Coke. To help us understand this contradiction, we can usefully divide the world into two types of products (marketers love to divide the world into two!), low and high involvement. *Low involvement goods*, Coke in the previous example, are ones which we don't think much about, we don't search for additional information, we generally buy on autopilot and we rarely feel buyer's remorse. They are generally regular repeat purchases and often are inexpensive. Once we settle on a choice we stick with it. *High involvement goods*, on the other hand tend to be infrequent purchases, are often expensive and we actively seek out information in order to make a better decision. A house or car, for most of us, are high involvement goods. An important aspect of high involvement goods from a marketer's viewpoint is that consumers are more apt to experience buyers remorse with high involvement goods. It is part of most people's human nature that after making an important decision is to wonder if we made a mistake. Clever marketers recognize this truth and often follow-up right after the sale or soon after with a message that reinforces the wisdom of the purchase in buying what they did. At IBM sales school, sales agents are taught to take the customer to lunch after they signed a multimillion-dollar computer contract. During the meal, the agent reminds the client the reasons they bought the product to encourage the client to realize they did in fact make the right decision. This may sound less than subtle but when done well it is quite effective. Research has shown that the most attentive viewers of new car ads are people who just bought the same car – they are seeking reinforcement that they got it right!

MODELS OF CONSUMER BEHAVIOUR

Having discussed the buyer decision process, we now turn our attention to modelling consumer behaviour. There are as many authors on the subject of consumer behaviour as there are models. In general they can be classified into two types: economic and psychological. Economic models assume buyers seek to satisfy their needs by maximizing the utility of their budget constraint. These buyers operate in conditions known as *perfect information*, which means all the information the buyer needs to make an informed decision is readily available. Though information is freely available in this world, money is not. As such, buyers in economic models weigh the potential benefits from various choices, and select those that maximize their *utility*. If the utility gained is more than expected, the customer is delighted. If it is less however, they will be disappointed and will readjust the value they ascribe to that product for future references.

While economic models provide satisfactory conclusions, the assumption of perfect information seems highly unlikely in practice. What's more, believing people carefully rationalize every decision is suspect; spontaneity is a human trait as well.

Psychological models assume that there are many different types of consumers, each influenced by different cultural, social and personal factors. Though more complex and harder to quantify, marketers generally prefer psychological models to explain consumer behaviour.

CULTURAL FACTORS

Culture according to the United Nations is the "set of distinctive spiritual, material, intellectual and emotional features of society or a social group, and that it encompasses, in addition to art and literature, lifestyles, ways of living together, value systems, traditions and beliefs". Since culture affects how a person sees and interacts with the world, it is the most important determinant in any psychological model.

Some of the key dimensions by which researchers understand culture are by the hierarchical distance in the society, that is the distance between those of high status and those of lower status, and the degree that the individual is important versus the group. Japan and Australia differ quite considerably on these important ways of understanding a culture. In Japan hierarchy and your position in society is important, Australia on the other hand is much more informal and relaxed, everyone is a "mate". In Japan group consensus is key to decision making and buying in the business-to-business marketing context. While in Australia one of their national symbols is the lone cowboy on the giant station or what Americans call a ranch, a potent metaphor of Australia's respect for the rugged individual.

One of the dangers of marketing outside of our home market is that we may well not understand how to effectively communicate a marketing message in that foreign culture. One lesson that many have learned is that they must hire people from that foreign culture to overcome cross-cultural differences. To complicate matters, within a national culture there are often distinct subcultures, Quebec in Canada is one example but even in the relatively homogeneous US market we can see that there are considerable cultural differences between New England, Texas, California and the Mid-West. The divisions do not end there. Within urban centres, distinct ethnic enclaves have emerged making it potentially difficult for marketers to use standard messages. Wal-Mart quite famously committed a considerable *faux pas* when it entered Canada in the 90s. Though a substantial percentage of the population speaks more than two languages, Wal-Mart put out door-to-door advertising only in English in Montreal, the second largest French speaking city in the world. Needless to say it took some years for Wal-Mart to win the hearts of Francophones in Montreal.

Marketers are always on the look out for shifts in cultural trends within a given country. During the 90s, consumers began to switch from fatty manufactured foods to low calorie and often organic foods. As the trend persisted, food manufacturers changed their entire marketing mix to reflect this new reality. Food giant Frito Lay for example launched a new version of their best selling potato chip using certified organic products and to reduce caloric content, used a baking process instead of deep-frying to prepare the food. To further separate the product from its unhealthier cousins, Baked Lays are often found in the organic section of a grocery store. Kraft Foods is following a similar course. Kraft Foods continues to develop single serve portion choices for some of its popular cheese, chocolate and savoury snack products. They have also introduced Nabisco 100 calorie packs, these are pre-portioned packages of Oreo Thin Crisps, Chips Ahoy! Thin Crisps, Kraft Cheese Nips and Wheat Thins Minis. What makes these products attractive is by being 100 calories, the consumer can easily track their calorie consumption, a challenge for many. Kraft is not the only vendor changing their product mix. McDonald's has added salads to their menu while Coca-Cola has bulked up their product line by selling water. When cultural trends change direction, business follows.

SOCIAL FACTORS

Psychological models also take into account social factors. Unless a person lives in total isolation, they belong to and are influenced by a number of **groups**. A group is two or more people who interact together for a common purpose. Because people in a group share a common purpose, it is assumed that their purchasing decisions are influenced by the attitudes and opinions of the most important people in the group. These opinion leaders are sometimes called **influencers**. Either with charisma, knowledge, special skills or a combination of these and other factors, influencers exert a considerable amount of sway on the opinions of the group. Marketers of consumer goods woo influencers to adopt their products because they are much more likely to convince **imitators** to also purchase the item. Athletic clothing manufacturers generously sponsor high-profile athletes because of their ability to influence tastes.

BUZZ MARKETING

In recent years, marketers have engaged in a practice called **buzz marketing** to woo imitators. Movies, books and CDs are all products which depend on a positive buzz to get people to buy them. Buzz marketing entails recruiting influencers to talk positively about a product to their friends. Gaining the endorsement of influencers creates with the masses, to use the official lingo, street cred. Buzz marketing is not always as seditious as it sounds. Sometimes the influencer promotes the product without resorting to direct coercion of neophytes. For example, search engine giant Google is the most successful company to date to successfully implement a buzz marketing strategy without the need to recruit influencers. Their search engine became the market leader with no marketing budget whatsoever because they successfully converted die hard Internet programmers into wilful promoters simply by offering a great product for fere and promising not to do evil. These individuals promoted the product to their peers and their friends for free.

CLASS STRUCTURE

A society's class structure is another group that influences choices. Though it might not seem apparent in some countries, class divisions exist in every society because the relationship between owners of production and those who actually do the work is inherently different. Social classes demonstrate distinct preferences when satisfying their needs. Those in the upper classes favour expensive brand name items because they offer an element of prestige and exclusivity. Whereas those in the lowest classes are extremely price sensitive. It is interesting to note that this may be changing. Unlike the past rich consumers are shopping at both Wal-Mart and Nordstrom's. On one hand, they want the cheap and cheerful offer of Wal-Mart for a substantial portion of their spending in order to save money and in concert with more traditional behaviour the rich, who can afford, also shop in top end shops. Interestingly, contrary to the past many lower income shoppers are shopping at Wal-Mart, no surprise there, but are also going upscale for some selected items. Their view appears to be, "we live more demanding, stressful, blackberry, cellphone, email beeping interrupted lives – we deserve some rewards!"

DEMOGRAPHICS

Another significant group that influences a person's choice is the demographic classification they were born into. In western nations, the population is divided into four distinct groups called **demographic cohorts**: Seniors (born in 1945 or earlier), Boomers (1946-1964), Generation X (1965-1985) and Generation Next (1986 to present).

Attitudes can vary considerably between one generation and the next. Take volunteerism for example. Boomers tend to be self-absorbed, more concerned with self-preservation than self-fulfilment, and are unable or unwilling to change the world. They are not without ambition or a sense of charity, but in their pursuit of self-fulfilment, career often crowds out family, and because volunteerism offers no serviceable rewards, it too is largely ignored. Meanwhile, Nexters have adopted a starkly different point of view towards volunteerism. This generation still under the age of 25 was raised in a multi-ethnic society, giving them an opportunity to view the world through the lens of a multicultural kaleidoscope. Unlike the

Boomers, they have a firmer understanding of the needs and characteristics of different socio-economic and cultural groups, motivating them to create a more caring society for both born and naturalized citizens. Nexters feel they must put something back into the well of society from which they had drawn.

Demographics are increasingly important for marketers to consider, this is especially true for Western Europe where birth rates are well below replace levels. For example, in Italy the birth rate of 1.23 children per woman, the second lowest in the Western world, this will have dramatic ramifications for Italian society, as fewer young people will be supporting a growing number of retirees. It also has implications for marketing in Italy; products which appeal to older people, reading glasses, golfing shoes, will be in greater demand and the need for baby clothes will decline.

PARENTS

Finally, the family a person belongs to also influences their choices. Parents play a crucial role in a child's development. Everything from the food the child eats to the value system the child adopts is influenced by parental decisions. Over time, the influence of parents decreases. Marketers have discovered that the "skirt tug" factor is increasingly playing a larger role in purchasing decisions. Perhaps because children are more adept at learning new technologies, it is the children who convince the parents that they need a new computer, DVD player or iPod.

PERSONAL FACTORS

Besides cultural and social factors, personal characteristics such as roles, occupation lifestyle and personality affect a buyer's choice. **Roles** are a set of activities a person is expected to perform in a particular social setting. The expected behaviours of a manager are very different than those of a parent, though one can be both. Each role a person adopts thus affects their purchasing decisions. A person's occupation is another factor to consider. Those who work in the construction industry require rugged, heavy-duty tools and clothing. What's more, they're likely to eat larger quantities of food ostensibly to replenish the nutrients they burn building our homes and office towers. A third factor that influences a buyer's choice is their lifestyle. **Lifestyle** is similar to culture in that it reflects a person's pattern of living and interacting with the world. Where it differs is that lifestyle choices are personal attitudes, and opinions, whereas cultural ones are imposed by society. Hip hop music started as a form of expressing the miseries of the black experience in America. Discrimination, lack of economic opportunities and violence are frequent themes in the music. Ironically, its commercial popularity today is due to droves of suburban white children who don't experience such a reality on a daily basis. Yet, many relate to the urban lifestyle, which includes baggy clothing, shiny jewellery and a colourful vocabulary. Finally, personality influences choice. **Personality** is usually described in terms of traits. Some traits include sociability, shyness, frugal, daring, sincerity, and self-confidence. By identifying a target market's personality traits, marketers can craft an appealing marketing mix. For example, daring individuals are likely to respond positively to an extreme vacation package.

RESEARCH METHODOLOGIES

Given the importance market research plays in decision making, what types of data and what means are used to collect data play a crucial role in the success of a product. This chapter takes a closer look at the four types of market research methodologies, quantitative, qualitative, observational, and experimental and discusses some key techniques like focus groups and shopping centre surveys.

QUANTITATIVE METHODS

4 out of 5 dentists recommend Crest. According to recent surveys of adult Australians there is a strong trend away from alcohol beverages and alcohol consumption in that country. These are examples of the results of quantitative research.

Quantitative methods are used to draw conclusions based on data collected from a group of customers chosen at random. Some common methods are surveys or questionnaires, you may well have run into market researchers at shopping centres stopping shoppers to ask them a set of questions. The aim of every quantitative study is to build a model that can predict the future with a high degree of accuracy. To start, the researcher must first observe a cause and effect relationship between two events. Let us assume a driver of an ice cream van noticed hordes of children, the children chased after him (driving at a very slow and safe speed of course) for blocks on end when the temperature was above 25 degrees Celsius. Once he stopped the van, a feeding frenzy would take place, as children practically begged him for larger sizes. However, when the temperature was cooler that 25 degrees, only those children who really wanted ice cream would make an effort. Leading the driver to conclude that the temperature is the difference between a bonanza and breaking even.

Is the driver correct? That's what quantitative models set out to prove one way or another using the principles of statistics, which believes if you observe a phenomenon long enough patterns will emerge. These patterns fall under a certain number of categories called **distributions**. Choose the right distribution, you then can accurately predict outcomes.

To build a quantitative model, a researcher would first express the relationship between ice cream sales and temperature mathematically in the form of a **null hypothesis**. A null hypothesis can be expressed as an equality, inequality or as the difference between two samples. A null hypothesis is also assumed to be true unless proven otherwise. The reason why statisticians assume the null is true is because it is much easier to disprove truth than proving it. Imagine you had an argument with a friend who claimed a particular fact was true. You had that sneaky suspicion in the back of your mind that perhaps your friend was stretching the truth. To see if that is indeed the case, you went on the computer, conducted a search on the Internet and discovered in fact your friend did misquote the fact. Statisticians love to disprove things as well, except they use mathematics.

Once the null hypothesis is stated, an appropriate test is chosen to determine the probability the null is indeed true. Choosing the test is not as difficult as it sounds. All you need is the sample size and the type of distribution. Under most cases, the distribution would be the standard bell shaped curve university students are familiar with. If the number of observations is below 30, then a **t-test** is used. If the number of observations is over 30, the appropriate test is called a **z-test**. Other types of distributions include exponential (used to model the growth rate of bacteria for example), poisson (no it does not measure the growth rate of fish, time periods actually), chi-squared and a host of others. For our purposes, we will restrict ourselves to normal distributions.

Once the appropriate test is chosen, the data is **normalized**. Now don't get confused between normal distribution and normalizing the data. Though the data can be modelled by a normal distribution it must first be transformed into a data set that will fit under the bell curve. The mathematics proving that the quality of the data is unaffected is well beyond the scope of this book, so take it for granted like the rest of us and assume it's true. With the data normalized, the researcher can now test if the null hypothesis is true by assigning a score to the data. This is done by subjecting the hypothesis to the most extreme cases possible, and seeing if the score lies under one of the tails of the curve. Statisticians call this area the alpha value. If the score does lie in that range, then you can safely conclude the null hypothesis is incorrect. If it does not, you do not conclude the null hypothesis is correct. Rather you conclude there is insufficient data to reject the null. Once the null has been determined not to be false (but not necessarily true), many more tests are needed to ensure the finding's reliability and validity. Repeating the test ensures no errors were made in collecting data, researchers unknowingly introduced a bias in the results or made other methodological mistakes. It takes a lot to convince a statistician something is true!

One final note about quantitative models. Even if a relationship between two variables is finally proven true using statistics, models can be manipulated. As Benjamin Disraeli, a 19th century Prime Minister of Great Britain once remarked, "there are lies, damn lies and statistics". Even today you can still read stories in the newspaper that claims a scientific study proves that one gender is better at logical problems than the other, or worse, one race is smarter than another. Our ice cream driver believes temperature affects ice cream sales, but forgets that if it is raining buckets outside, even if it's 30 degrees Celsius outside, very few will make the effort to run for their ice cream.

QUALITATIVE METHODS

Qualitative methods takes the opposite approach to quantitative ones. Whereas numbers are needed in quantitative, a qualitative model relies on a direct approach: subjects are asked questions to gain a sense of their opinions. Qualitative models are useful because they explain to the marketer why things are the way they are (academics would characterize them as **normative**), as opposed to quantitative models which are **prescriptive** or describe how things should be. Quantitative research is done when you have a theory or one or more hypothesis to test, qualitative takes place before you have a theory, it is more exploratory, seeking to understand the broad outlines of a question. Thus, usually, qualitative studies are conducted first and then followed by a quantitative study to confirm the hypothesis generated from the qualitative study. The next section discusses some of the more popular qualitative research methods.

FOCUS GROUPS

Focus groups are popular with marketers, especially when they're trying to find out exactly what their customers' needs are. It entails inviting a small group of people (usually a group between 8 to 12) who comprise a good representation of the target market. A moderator then asks the group questions to discuss their opinions about how the product satisfies or fails their needs. Once a discussion starts, the moderator somewhat removes themselves from the discussion, letting the participants debate amongst themselves. From time to time the moderator interrupts to get the discussion back on track. The session usually lasts for an hour, and is taped. Later, researchers transcribe the event and analyse the text to gauge each member's opinions and attitudes.

The problem with focus groups is that it is vulnerable to group dynamics. In every group there is pressure to conform to one opinion. Because the discussion is free flowing, in theory at least, everyone has an equal voice. Yet if there is a charismatic or extremely vocal person forcibly expressing their opinions, in the interest of "moving on" most people will yield if they perceive the effort to be far more than the satisfaction of winning. A good moderator should be able to spot such a situation and intervene. On the other hand, moderators can hamper the quality of the research.

Studies have shown that moderators can bias the group into saying what the researchers want to hear simply by asking leading questions, which is a form of questioning where the answer is included in the question. If you ever watch an interview with a sports figure, the interviewer nearly always asks a leading question, much like the following: "the rain played havoc with the field conditions, how hard was it to play on the pitch tonight?" Even if the moderator is given a standard set of questions, the subjects themselves might give answers the researchers want to hear without being prompted. Many times the subjects are compensated for their time. As such, some feel they owe it to the funder to give them what they want. Clearly, focus groups are useful, but due to inherent flaws in the test, it shouldn't be regarded as the sole means of gauging buyer opinions.

INTERVIEWS

Interviews are one-on-one situations where an interviewer asks a subject direct and often probing questions. A person's preferences, belief system and attitudes along with their opinions can be learned without the worries of conforming to a group. Interviewing is a very useful method if the person interviewed is an expert or someone who represents a large group. What's more, the interview is largely unstructured, making the whole interview seem more like a conversation than a formal question and answer period. If the right source is found, a wealth of information can be extracted. One interview project Karl worked on was to interview people about their use of green or environmentally friendly products. This was for a large Canadian supermarket, Loblaws, which in the 90s introduced a large number of green products in their stores based on the fact that Canadians in survey after survey agree they would pay more for a greener product. Unfortunately, these products weren't selling well. In order to understand better this dichotomy, interviews were used. They were conducted in the home of the informants and involved rummaging through the refrigerator and under the kitchen sink, rather odd behaviour! The net result was that the research concluded that Canadians wanted, contrary to the quantitative research, products that got their clothes "just as white", were better for the environment, but cost no more! This is entirely unfair but there you have the explanation why they were not buying the green products. Why did quantitative research not catch this? Because people wanted to please the nice interviewer at their door or on the phone and because it would be politically incorrect to say the truth of the matter.

Unfortunately, finding a good source is difficult. Not all goods have trend and taste setters who lead the way. Successful interviews also require having good interviewers. Listening, believe it or not is a difficult skill because it entails trying to understand what the other person is really saying and then adjusting manner in which the questions are asked to mirror the other person's manner of thinking. Barbara Walters of ABC is one of the few journalists who can do such a thing. If you watch enough of her interviews, you will notice that within the first five minutes of an interview, she is asking probing questions that sound as if she's agreeing with the interviewee, but in reality she is maintaining her distance and objectivity. It is a remarkable skill. And as we all know what is remarkable is difficult to replicate. Finding another Barbara Walters is not easy, and also, not cheap.

ASSOCIATION TECHNIQUES

Association techniques are used to determine a person's beliefs or attitudes towards an issue or product. The difference here is that projective techniques attempt to disguise the purpose of the research by telling the subject the study is studying a different phenomenon. It is also used with children who may have not have the verbal skills to do an interview and for topics where people's thoughts are not very well formed, but the researcher wants to explore their feelings and thinking below the surface about a product. The idea is that the subject will then give answers that they do believe rather than what researchers want to hear, which can happen in interviews and focus group settings. Subjects are asked to participate in such activities as **word association** games, complete an unfinished sentence, role-play, or complete a Rorschach test. Marketers like using association techniques to gauge consumer familiarity towards a brand's slogan. One example is to ask what furniture would be found in the Heineken living room? Or in the Corona living room, what sport is on the television? Though we may not think about beer a lot the marketer researcher is trying to surface the sub-conscious thoughts and feeling they have about various beer brands. Children may be asked to finish a simple story or fill in a bubble in a cartoon with what the person is saying.

Catching the subject off-guard can yield interesting answers if the conclusions are restricted to the "isn't this interesting?" category. What we mean by that is too often marketers over-analyse data. It is as if they feel compelled to uncover new discoveries because they are conducting a scientific study. What they fail to remember is that in every scientific study you have to control the environment in order to replicate the results consistently. In the social sciences, that's very difficult to do, which means you have to cut out some details that you hope are not important. There are many examples of over-analysis. Perhaps the most famous involved Sigmund Frued and one of his students. One day Freud told his student that the night before he had dreamt about cigars. Nothing but cigars. Now, most of us would shrug our shoulders and say that's nice, and start to inch our way to the door hoping to escape before he continues to tell the rest of his dull dream. However, to a student of the world's most famous psycho-analyst, a dream about a cigar is explicit proof that the cigar is actually a metaphor for a repressed desire to engage in homosexu-ality. To which Freud remarked, "Sometimes a cigar is just a cigar".

OBSERVATIONAL METHODS

Observational methods are techniques that (no surprise here) involve the researcher observing the subject in question in its natural setting. Observational methods are useful because researchers are pretty confident that their influence is nullified in the outcome of the study. One example is to go to a Man United game in order to understand what the fans experience. The drawback is that since the researcher remains on the sidelines, they cannot replicate the outcome easily. Any photographer will tell you it was the day they left their camera at home the perfect shot presented itself.

Observational techniques are used heavily in conducting market research. Ratings agency Nielson attaches a box to participant's television sets, tracking their channel preferences. In addition, many use tools to measure a subject's pulse, eye-movement and eventually brain-scans to test their reaction to a product. Less invasive means of observing consumers is to use cameras to track buying patterns. Credit card companies track and analyse your purchasing habits each time you swipe your card. Computer companies leave cookies on your computer to track which websites you visit. Observational methods can infringe on an individual's sense of freedom.

EXPERIMENTAL METHODOLOGIES

Experimental methodologies attempt to create semi-isolated environments that are similar to the real world. The idea is that by creating a model world, many of the extraneous factors are eliminated thus giving the researcher a good idea of the real cause-and-effect relationship between variables. Test markets are a great example of this. In a test market setting, a new product is launched in a small sized city with a population that is representative for the whole market. Researchers modify each P at a time to determine the best mix.

Another new type of testing that is happening in the marketplace is the emergence of scenario testing using simulators. The rapidly declining cost of computing power along with the emergence of programmers who realize that technology is meant to make our lives easier, the creation of a virtual market using data collected from the field has become more and more prevalent. One of the neat advantages of using a computer is that it can crunch millions of bits of information quickly. As we mentioned earlier, to get a good sense of how consumers behave, you need to do lots of studies from a variety of perspectives. By using a computer, you can incorporate the findings into one place, and also incorporate market dynamics to simulate how changes in the business environment affect sales. Once you build the program, you can do virtually anything you please. Want to see how your product reacts in an inflationary period with hyper-adaptive competitors? With a simulator you can find out.

The main reason a marketer would want to use a simulator is for planning purposes. Asking a manager to predict the future is impossible. However ask a manager what they should do if their competitor just introduced a new product that seems to catch the imagination of the market, you'd get a much better answer. That is where the simulator comes in. By creating virtual worlds, managers can create contingency plans just in case the proverbial doo doo hits the fan. By having the plans in place, managers will not be caught off guard and forced to react to uncertainty. By anticipating the problem, steps can be taken to mitigate the uncertainty. Simulators are starting to get the attention of military planners. Electronic Arts makers of the popular software game called *The Sims* has a contract with the US military to create virtual worlds. The idea is to see how the chain of command is effected if some calamity struck. Each officer is given a personality, rank and set of orders. By tweaking the scenario rules, planners can assess the effectiveness of their policies under conditions of a nuclear or biological attack. Of course, the key is creating the right model. If the code that models the dynamics between people, products and the market does not reflect reality, the contingency plans are practically useless.

One final note about simulators. A phenomenon that has been around for many years but has recently caught the attention of marketers are **massive multiplayer online games (MMOG)**. These are programs which a person can download on their computer and pay a monthly fee to participate in a virtual world with tens of thousands of other players. What makes these games so interesting is that while some participants join to engage in escapism (often in the form of hacking monsters to pieces with a battleaxe), some subscribers take up a craft and sell their virtual wares. Every daring adventurer needs weapons, clothing, food and a place to sleep and network to hear the latest rumours about a king's ransom guarded by a dragon. So some players have decided to cater to those needs by creating virtual goods that do just that. And because the service is restricted to subscribers, it is easy to attribute a cause to observed changes. For example, hackers of one MMOG managed to exploit a flaw which essentially enabled them to mint their own money. Predictably the influx of this new money led to an inflation of prices. MMOGs are a virtual economy filled with self-aware participants acting in a normal manner, some are self-interested, others selfless. Companies that sell MMOGs may not have realized at the time, but they might have created the ideal testing ground for conducting market research.

AN EMERGING APPROACH – NEUROMARKETING

The field of marketing research marches onward year after year, new techniques, new approaches. When garbology first came out, many found much amusement in the idea of rooting through someone's garbage in order to better understand their consumption patterns. Today, it is much more accepted, though still assigned to more junior market researchers. A type of marketing research which has recently garnered considerable attention is neuromarketing. What particularly set off this interest was a study published in the Oct. 14, 2004 issue of *Neuron*. Researchers monitored brain-scans of 67 people who were given a blind taste test of Coca-Cola and Pepsi. Using brain-scanners they could see that each soft drink "lit up" the brain's reward system. Participants were evenly split about which drink they preferred. However, when the same people were told what they were drinking, activity in a different set of brain regions were engaged. Three out of four said they preferred Coca-Cola. This demonstrated in a fairly dramatic way that brand matters.

Marketers have long regarded the human mind as a **black box**. We marketers do our thing: beaming advertising, direct marketing pieces, a sales pitch or what have you to our target market. We can measure the results of that marketing effort, in terms of sales, awareness, liking, etc. We understand reasonably well the beginning and end of the process but not the vital part in the middle. That is, what goes on inside the mind of the consumer. This is what is changing with neuromarketing. First, the basic fundamental science underlying neuromarketing is neuroscience, which is the study of the how the brain gives rise to the mind. In other words how the brain enables us to perceive, think, make decisions, feel emotions, communicate (i.e., the neural basis of human experience). Techniques used by neuroscience are: psychophysics (reaction times/detection levels), functional magnetic resonance imaging (FMRI), magnetoencephalography (MEG) and electroencephalography (EEG).

The most interesting of these to neuromarketing is FMRI scanning. I am sure we all have seen these on *ER* or other television shows, where the patient is slid inside a machine which hums and makes various other noises. Neuromarketing is the application of the techniques of neuroscience to marketing stimuli, in layman's terms, to see how the brain "lights up" when exposed to our marketing efforts. Science has made a great deal of progress in understanding our brains. Many called the 90s the "decade of the brain" and in the last 20 years there have been more than 100,000 scientific publications on this most complex of organs.

It is early days for neuroscience, but what research has been done has stirred up a considerable amount of interest in the idea of neuromarketing. It is being touted by some as the next big thing. If marketers can use science to locate consumers' "buy buttons", then we have gotten closer to opening the **black box** of the consumer's mind. The best use of neuromarketing is in predicting behaviour, spotting the advertisements that people remember, selecting the media format that works best and how what consumers actually do differs from what they tell focus groups. Other uses I have seen or read about include reactions to movie trailers, choices about automobiles, the appeal of a pretty face and visceral reactions to political campaign advertising.

Neuromarketing has critics. We share some of their fears; it raises the possibility of a too useful tool for Big Brother being one of them. Other concerns include the costs and the unpleasantness of a scan. Dr. Gemma Calvert, co-founder of Neurosense Ltd., a neuro-marketing consultancy, noted in a recent issue of the London *Times*: "MRI (magnetic resonance imaging) is not as expensive as people think and is only slightly more expensive than the average cost of conducting focus groups . . . and OK, it is not pleasant, but it isn't unpleasant either. We have never had a problem getting people into scanners; most have read about brain imaging and are really keen to have a go".

At this point brain-scanning is being used as an adjunct to traditional market research techniques, including focus groups. In the future, perhaps 5 to 10 years off at this point, I think brain-scanning may well become a routine part of corporate marketing strategies.

CONCLUSION

Qualitative methods are favoured by marketers due to their low cost. After observing a casual relationship between a number of variables, a quantitative study is launched to test to see if the relationship is in fact statistically significant. If significance is determined, then the marketer should adjust the marketing mix to reflect this reality. In order to collect data, observational and association techniques are used. Group dynamics issues, bias, and naturally cost all play a factor in deciding which methods should be used. Today due to the decline in cost of computing power, simulators are starting to creep into the planning process as it provides a useful means of contingency planning. Eventually neuromarketing will have a place in the manager's toolkit, but its promises are still a few years away.

SUMMARY

- The stimulus-response model is a basis from which to analyse consumer behaviour.
- Culture, social, personal factors all contribute to the purchasing decision.
- Leaders of a group influence the group's tastes.
- Analysing demographic preferences provides insights about future trends.
- Marketers use a variety of qualitative, quantitative and other methods to learn what drives the purchasing decision.
- Rapid advances in computing and brain-imaging technology are opening new horizons in marketing.

CRITICAL QUESTIONS

1. Which demographic cohort do you belong to? What would you say are your personal values? Do they match those exhibited by your demographic?
2. List the major factors that affect buyer behaviour. Which factors do you think are losing influence and which do you think are gaining influence? Are there factors that are missing?
3. List the stages of the buyer decision process. Is the process applicable for every product? How can taste-setters influence the process? What makes a taste-setter so special?
4. What are the advantages and disadvantages of using (a) focus groups, (b) interviews, and (c) association techniques?
5. What are the ethical implications of using neuromarketing?
6. What are the advantages and disadvantages of using simulators to build virtual economies?

SUGGESTIONS FOR FURTHER READING

Al Ries and Laura Ries, *The Fall of Advertising and the Rise of PR*, New York, Harper Collins, 2004.

A father and daughter team discuss the rise of buzz and how to use it in your business.

Emanuel Rosen, *The Anatomy of Buzz: How to Create Word of Mouth Marketing*, New York, Currency, 2002.

The first big book on buzz marketing, this is an excellent foundational read for anyone trying to get a handle on buzz.

Leon Schiffman and Leslie Kanuk, *Consumer Behaviour*, Eighth Edition, New Jersey, Prentice Hall, 2003.

A textbook which has proven itself over 8 editions, it gives you all you need to and want to know about consumer behaviour.

Geert Hofstede, *Culture's Consequences: Comparing Values, Behaviours, Institutions and Organizations Across Nations*, 2nd edition, New York, Sage, 2003.

A fascinating book that looks at the differences across cultures.

GLOSSARY

Black box A term used to describe the process which a buyer undergoes when making a purchasing decision.

Buyer decision process A five stage process that a buyer passes through when making a purchase.

Buyer's remorse See post purchase behaviour.

Buzz marketing A promotion technique that relies on influencers to speak highly of a product.

Consumer behaviour The buying behaviour of consumers.

Culture The set of distinctive spiritual, material, intellectual and emotional features of society or a social group, and that it encompasses, in addition to art and literature, lifestyles, ways of living together, value systems, traditions and beliefs.

Demographic cohort A group of people born in a particular time.

Distribution A word describing the arrangement of a series of data plotted on a graph.

Evaluation of alternatives   The evaluation of the potential benefits against the potential drawbacks from making one purchasing choice over another.

Groups   Two or more people interacting together for a common purpose.

Lifestyle   A manner of living reflected in a person's personal opinions, values and choices.

Imitator   A person who adopts the habits of an influencer.

Influencer   A person who wields influence over a group.

Information search   The second stage of the buyer decision process whereby the buyer seeks out information in order to make an informed purchasing decision.

Massive Multiplayer Online Games (MMOG)   A computer game that enables hundreds of thousands of users to interact within a simulated world via the Internet.

Need recognition   The first stage of the buyer decision process whereby the buyer realizes they have an unsatisfied need.

Normalized   A method of transforming data in order to apply various statistical tests.

Normative   The way things are.

Null hypothesis   A hypothesis assumed to be true until proven otherwise.

Perceived performance   The implied performance level of a product as expressed in a product's promotional mix.

Perfect information   A theoretical environment whereby consumers have access to any source of information needed to make an informed decision.

Personality   The sum of qualities and traits, that are particular to a person.

Post-purchase behaviour   The customer's reaction to their purchase decision.

Prescriptive   The way things should be.

Purchase decision   The product selected to satisfy a need.

Role   A set of activities a person is expected to perform in a particular social setting.

T-Test   A test applied a null hypothesis claiming a sample size of less than 30 is a t-distribution.

Utility   The level of satisfaction a consumer receives from making a choice.

Word association   A type of analysis where the tester prompts the subject for an immediate answer to uncover what types of associations the subject has made with a product.

Z-Test   A test applied a null hypothesis claiming a sample size of more than 30 is a z-distribution.

9

GLOBAL MARKETING

INTRODUCTION

The World Is Flat is the title of a recent best selling book by *New York Times* Columnist Thomas Freidman and pundit on globalization. Perhaps he does get a bit carried away but certainly if not flat the world is certainly much more accessible to marketers today than twenty years ago. This is a two-edged sword – we get to sell in other countries but they also get to turn up the competitive heat for us in our home markets. Not that we have much of a choice – foreign competitors are increasingly the reality. In this chapter we will focus on the opportunity that competing in foreign markets offers.

FIRST DECISIONS

The starting point for firms seriously considering whether they should market outside their home country is whether they have more attractive opportunities still available in their home market before they go to the considerable cost of going elsewhere, and it is expensive to market elsewhere. We'll talk more about those costs shortly. So the first question is why go overseas? We call it overseas even if it is next door like, a German firm selling in France, where clearly there is no sea involved, English expressions, go figure. The most common reason is that you have saturated your home market and additional growth will be expensive to achieve. Most firms can always grow but the cost of achieving an additional 1% of market share may be prohibitive. Another big reason to compete elsewhere is from a view of better understanding your key foreign competitors so that you can better compete against them in your home market, which for many firms tend to remain the dominant market for many decades. Some big multinationals firms, like Nokia, Hitachi and BMW are no longer dominated by their home markets and become even more international in their outlook over time. But in this case we are thinking about the smaller firm just starting out. Other reasons might include, needing a larger customer base to achieve economies of scale, wanting to diversify your risk which comes from being too dependent on one market, and customers going abroad and wanting you to service them there.

Once you have decided that you should seriously consider foreign markets the next question is which foreign market do you start with? For firms in some countries the choices are fairly obvious. For a Canadian firm the US is the natural place to go. For Mexican firms the US as well. This is due not only to the physical closeness but also economic treaties and what is called **psychic** or **cultural proximity**. Not only do the US and Canada share borders but they are also culturally quite similar. When most Canadians travel in the US they are assumed to be fellow Americans by Americans. We tend to feel more comfortable in culturally similar countries but more importantly we tend to be more successful marketing to cultures which we naturally seem to understand. In Europe it is not quite as obvious where you should first go. Take for example, the Netherlands, the Dutch are quite flexible, because of their history, culture and language skills. The Dutch tend to be able to export to Germans, French, Belgians, Danes and Britons with equal ease. Part of this ease is the reality that there is only a little over 16 million Dutch people. At a certain point in your success as a Dutch firm you run out of Dutch people! Then you naturally turn to your neighbours for growth. This helps explain why Nokia, the cellphone maker, had to naturally start exporting early in their history, there are fewer Finns, about 5 million.

This naturally raises the question, why do we care about growth? Some firms where the owner and founder is getting on in years and may not care, they are just waiting it out till retirement and enjoying the income which flows from years of hard work. However for publicly traded companies or for firms with younger owners growth is a necessity. The stock market looks to firms for regular growth, year in, year out, if they don't deliver their stock price will decline which if it goes on too long will mean a cry for a new CEO.

Other things to consider when you are thinking about which market to enter first is have we had multiple requests from the country for our product. Often first export sales occur often almost by serendipity. A firm from another country hears about our products and calls to order. For many the initial reaction is go away, don't bother us, it is too much work to send our product to you. One of these foreign firms just keep working on us, perhaps offering a considerable price premium to service them, we break down and do. Humble beginnings but many a large firm has started out this way.

HOW TO ENTER THE COUNTRY OR MODE OF ENTRY

Once a firm decides to target a particular country it has to decide the best mode of entry. That is should it indirectly export, directly export, license its product to another firm, form a joint venture or use direct investment. This is a critical decision which we will spend some time on next. Over time as the firms enjoys or doesn't enjoy success it may well evolve in an intelligent design from one form to a more committed form. Firms often start with more of a toe in the water approach by only indirectly exporting, the form which takes the least commitment and resources, but as they do well move to a more committed form of international activity.

INDIRECT AND DIRECT EXPORT

This is the normal starting place for most firms. **Occasional exporting** is a relatively passive phase which we talked about earlier where the firm exports from time to time almost under protest. **Active exporting** takes place when the firm makes a commitment to expand into a particular market or markets. Companies typically start with indirect exporting, that is they use independent intermediaries.

Domestic-based export merchants buy the vendor's products and then sell them on their behalf abroad. **Domestic-based export agents** seek and negotiate foreign purchases on your behalf and are paid on commission. **Cooperative organizations** carry on exporting activities on behalf of a number of producers and are typically partly under their control. Producers of primary products such as fruits, nuts or maple syrup, often use them. One example is the BC Tree Fruit Marketing Board which helps sell various fruits that comes from trees in British Columbia around the world. In Australia there are many marketing cooperatives including the Australian Fresh Mango Co-operative Ltd, Shepherds Producers Co-operative Ltd and the Goat Meat Producers Co-operative Ltd to name just a few. OPEC is another example. Though members are nation states, they all sell to the same global market.

Indirect export has two principle advantages. Firstly, less investment because the firm does not have to set up an export department, overseas sales force or international contact network which needs care and feeding. Secondly, it means less risk, because of the know-how and experience of these intermediate firms the firm will generally make fewer costly mistakes.

Over time, with success, firms often decide to directly move to handle their own exports. Risk is higher but so is the potential for greater profitability and as your experience with indirect export grows so does your confidence that you don't need anybody else's help. There are several different ways to go about direct exporting:

- Domestic-based export department or division.
- Travelling export sales reps. Get them out on the road.
- Overseas sales branch or subsidiary. This is closer to the customer and gives the opportunity to better tailor products to the differing needs of foreign customers.
- Foreign-based distributors or agents. They may be given the exclusive rights to report the company in a given country or countries or only limited rights – something to negotiate over.

Many firms will eventually move to direct on-the-ground investment but they will use the above methods to "test the water".

THE INTERNET

We would be remiss if we did not mention the web and international marketing. One of the key ways many firms have traditionally gotten started overseas is through overseas trade shows. These big trade shows are often scheduled a year or two ahead of time and repeated every year. The shows bring thousands of potential buyers and sellers together for the very purpose of connected manufacturers and firms that can help them export to their market. These days the web is also an interesting strategy to reach customers outside your home market.

San Francisco based upscale retailer, The Sharper Image, according to the august *Wall Street Journal*, now gets more than 28% of its online business from overseas customers. The biggest place for online orders is flagship website sharperimage.com which mainly serves the home market of the US. It also operates 10 other sites for markets worldwide. Included among the 10 is a Spanish-language version of its US site that's used by consumers in Mexico and Latin America as well as by Spanish-speaking people in the US. The other sites are designed for the UK, Germany, Australia, Hong Kong, China, Japan, Singapore and Taiwan, with a separate site for the European Union. According to press reports, to expedite shipping and returns in its busiest foreign markets – several European countries – Sharper Image maintains a distribution centre in Rotterdam, Netherlands, for returns as well as deliveries.

Another of the world's big catalogue and Internet retailers is Lands' End, headquarters in Dodgeville, Wisconsin. According to a 2005 article in *Time*, Lands' End created French and Italian versions of its American website in 2004. Says Sam Taylor, vice president of Lands' End international operations: "There's a feeling we want to come through in the copywriting when it's translated". For a women's gingham-check swimsuit, marketed to French customers, consultant Berlitz modified the catalogue copy to read, *"L'effet B.B. assure!"* (the B.B. look guaranteed!), a reference to Brigitte Bardot, who made gingham fashionable in the 50s. Within a decade, Lands' End forecasts, 35% to 45% of revenues will be generated abroad.

These examples demonstrate that for well-known brands getting people to visit their website is less of a task, foreigners will start visiting. Smaller firms are in a less enviable position of not having people naturally seek them out on the web. They will still find that if they do well in their particular niche, word will spread and some foreign potential customers will find you out on the web. Then the question is how do you service them? The great thing about the web that it knows no barriers, other than language and it can be accessed from anywhere in the world that has a computer and an Internet connection. Once foreign orders start what will you do? Reject them outright or allow them if they accept delivery in your home country only? If you want to take advantage of them you almost certainly need to do what Lands' End did, that is set up national or at least regional centres to service them and adopt your product to their language and culture. I say both language and culture because though England shares the English language with the US, Australia etc., you still need to use some different words, petrol rather than gas, etc., but also a good marketer will use local expressions, local icons, etc., to effectively e-market in that particular market.

LICENSING

Licensing is a simple and relatively easy way to get involved in international marketing. The licensor issues a license to a foreign company to use a manufacturing process, trademark, patent, trade secret, or some other item of value for a fee or royalty payment. The licensee gains product expertise, a well-known product or brand, or some other knowledge or right it would be expensive to obtain, while the licensor gains entry into a new market with little risk. There are, like anything in life, strengths and weaknesses. The weaknesses are very real and must be taken account of. The licensor has less control over the licensee than it does over its own employees. And if the licensee is quite successful the firm has given up considerable profit and may have created its own competition when the contract ends. One way to avoid this is do what Coke does and provide a key proprietary ingredient or part vital to the product. However, the best strategy is for the licensor to be an innovation leader keeping ahead of the pack thus having the licensee to continue to be dependent on the licensor.

There are several variations on this theme. The Four Seasons company sells management contracts to owner of hotels in many parts of the world to manage their hotels for a fee. **Contract manufacturing** is where a firm hires local manufacturers to produce the product. Many firms will use a local firm to manufacture within Mexico for example to produce products appropriate for their needs. A newer phenomenon is the idea of outsourcing your manufacturing entirely to a firm, often foreign with plants in various parts of the world to allow you to focus on other parts of your business where your firm can contribute more value. In Nike's case, designing the sports shoes, building and working with their brand equity and marketing the brand. Another interesting example is, KeyTronicEMS a Spokane Washington based firm which offers customers a complete global manufacturing solution. They have plants in the US, Mexico and China. These facilities provide their customers the opportunity to manufacture in the facility that best serves specific product manufacturing and distribution needs.

JOINT VENTURES

Foreign firms may join with local investors to create a join venture (JV) firm in which they share ownership and control. A joint venture may be necessary for political and economic reasons. The foreign firm may lack the financial, physical, market knowledge or managerial resources to undertake the venture alone or the foreign government might require joint ownership as a condition to do business in their country. This has been the experience of many firms seeking to enter the vast Chinese market. At one time it was a legal requirement to have a foreign part, that has been largely eliminated (though it is still required in telecoms at the time of the writing of this book). But even large multinationals like European food giant Unilever often enter into joint ventures in China in order to get the local investors to help with the at times horrendous Chinese bureaucracy and putting a more local face on the venture. Other advantages a Chinese partner may bring include central or local government support, brand reputation, land, licences, distribution, and access to suppliers, which reduce start up costs and improve the foreign investor's chances of success. JVs have their drawbacks. First, since all JV contract details need to be negotiated, establishing a JV is often quite time consuming and expensive. Indeed, JV negotiations can derail potential ventures as parties discover that they cannot reach agreement on important points. Secondly, JVs mean you have to share the profits with partners and finally you have to share decision making which means that you cannot do things the way you want nor can you have globally consistent manufacturing and marketing policies.

FOREIGN DIRECT INVESTMENT

The ultimate in foreign involvement is foreign direct investment of FDI. This is where your firm owns manufacturing or assembly facilities in another country. The foreign company can have part or full interest in a local company or build its own facilities. Auto giant GM has invested billions of dollars over decades in auto manufacturers around the world, including China's Shangai GM and Jinbei GM; Italy's Fiat; Japan's Isuzu and Suzuki; Korea's Kaewoo, Suzuki; Sweden's Saab, and AvtoVAZ of Russia. If the market is large enough warrant this type of entry, foreign production facilities offer some real advantages. Firstly, the firm enjoys cost savings in terms of cheaper labour or raw materials, foreign government investment incentives if they exist and they often do, and transportation savings since you are much closer to the customer.

There are further advantages of FDI; for example, the firm tends to enjoy a better image in the host country with government and customers alike. Wal-Mart and MacDonald's both well-known US firms try to do this abroad. Wal-Mart bought ASDA in the UK, Seiyu in Japan, and Woolco in Canada in order to create a local presence quickly. In the UK and Japan they continued to trade under the names of the firms they bought. In Canada they have sought to Canadianize Wal-Mart as much as possible so it begins to seem like another Canadian firm to Canadian customers. Another advantage is that the firm can build a deeper relationship with customers, local suppliers and the distribution system of the country. This is quite helpful in adapting their products to the particular needs of that country. Also, the company retains control over its investment and can implement global standards in manufacturing and marketing policies. Finally the firm is assured of market access in that country in case the host country government starts insisting on locally produced content. The primary disadvantage of FDI is that if the government goes wonky you may be stuck with a large investment with exposure to issues like blocked or devalued currencies, terrible markets or even expropriation. Of these risks the most likely to happen is currency fluctuations which can impact overall corporate profitability a great deal.

ADOPTING THE MARKETING PROGRAM

There is one simple diagram which captures a central issue in international marketing, please see Figure 9.1. This figure captures a key tension in international marketing, how much do we leave the product unchanged versus how much do we adapt for local tastes? If we change any part of the marketing mix it causes additional expense, this is captured on the X-axis. So we argue for a one product, one promotion, one price, etc., world. The advantages are multifold, economies of scale in production and distribution, and lower marketing costs because we use one ad for the world. Consistency in brand image is critical because we live in a world that watches each other's television and travels to each other's country. Another benefit is the ability to lever good ideas quickly and efficiently across **lead markets**.

However, the reality is that foreign cultures are often different from our own, so we must adjust the marketing mix in order to

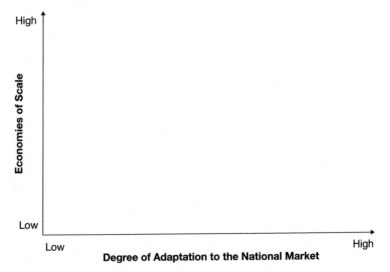

Figure 9.1   How Much do You Adapt the Product to the Local Market?

have a product which customers in that culture will want to buy. The difference can be multifold. Differences in consumer needs, wants and usage patterns for products. Nowhere is this truer than in developing countries where one hit product is a radio that you wind to power it, much like an alarm clock – not a product that would be much of a winner in a market in Western Europe. Differences in consumer response to marketing mix elements and differences in the legal environment and the marketing institutions. For example in Canada when you advertise pharmaceutical products you can either mention the disease or the drug name but not both, in the US you can mention both, thus ads for the same product must, by law, be different for the two countries.

Some products, like Sony televisions or Dell computers don't need too much adaptation, consumers around the world are looking for not dissimilar offerings. At the other extreme are local foods which can vary considerably. A favourite restaurant of mine in Tokyo offers only dishes made from cow tongues. Clearly, they have found a niche market, and given the line up to get in on a Saturday night an excellent one. However, this particular Japanese cuisine, unlike Sushi, doesn't seem to export well to other nations. For the marketer figuring out the degree to which culture is important and the degree to which they should go for one world product and marketing mix is a critical decision. Lets now go through the marketing mix to quickly consider each in turn in how a marketer may have to fine tune for different foreign markets. But before we do that a few thoughts on culture.

NATIONAL CULTURE

To anyone who has travelled it is obvious that cultures differ. That is part of the charm of Europe where many cultures are crowed into a fairly small area. In parts of Holland you can not only eat in a German, Belgium or Dutch restaurant you can actually get those countries within an hour or so drive. Dutch researcher Geert Hofstede identified four cultural dimensions that can differentiate nations.

- Individualism versus collectivism. In more collective societies, like Japan, the self-worth of the individual is rooted more in the group than in individual achievement. How different than America. Does your country have the expression that "the tall Poppy gets it's head cut off"?

- Masculine versus feminine. This uses traditional female/ male definitions but still most people get the gist of it which is the degree that the culture is dominated by assertive males versus more nurturing female values. Is it all right to show uncertainty with a decision?

- High versus low power distance. Low power distance cultures tend to be more egalitarian. The Nordic countries are low power distance cultures where there is not a great deal of difference between the top and the bottom ranks of society. Do you call your boss Sir or Madam?

- Weak versus strong uncertainty avoidance. This is about how risk tolerant or adverse people are. Does your stomach tighten when you have some risk or do you have lots of entrepreneurs in your society?

Virtually all products have to undergo some changes in produce features, packaging, channels, pricing or communications, the marketing mix as they strive to be successful in different world markets.

PRODUCT

When the Walt Disney company launched EuroDisney outside Paris in 1992 it thought it had a real winner right out of the starting gate. After all, Tokyo Disneyland was an almost exact clone of the mother ship Disneyland in California and it was a huge success. However, they quickly recognized that it was not going to work the same in Europe. After years of tweaking the park they finally ended up with Europe's biggest tourist attraction, after much Europeanizing and rebranding under the name Disneyland Paris. What the Japanese wanted was a day in America when they visited Disney Tokyo what Europeans wanted was more complex and considerable changes to the product were made before success finally arrived.

Global marketing guru, Warren Keegan suggests three overall adaptation strategies of product and communications for foreign markets: please see Figure 9.2.

Figure 9.2   Communications Adaptation Model

		Product		
		Do Not Change Product	*Adapt Product*	*Develop New Product*
Communications	*Do Not Change Communications*	Straight Extension	Product Adaptation	
	Adapt Communications	Communication Adaptation	Dual Adaptation	Product Invention

1   **Straight Extension** means introducing the product in the foreign market without changing the product mix. The potentially seductive thing about straight extensions is that the producer does not incur additional R&D, manufacturing or promotion modifications. This approach has been used with consumer electronics, cameras on the consumer side and big industrial tools on the B2B side. At other times straight extensions have failed miserably. Campbell soups lost an estimated $30 million US when it unsuccessfully introduced its condensed soups in the UK. Managers must also be wary of exporting their product where the product's name has an entirely different meaning. Evite.com is a website that among others, allows users to send invitations to social events. In French, the word *evite*, is a conjugation of the verb *eviter*, which means to avoid. Needless to say, Evite.com does not have a French version of their site.

2   **Product Adaptation** involves altering the product to meet local preferences or conditions. Warren suggests several levels of adaptation.

   • A firm can produce a regional version of its product, such as a North American version. We are seeing an increasing number of North American and European products which are offered throughout the countries of those regions. In North America the packaging would be in the major languages of the region, English, Spanish and French. This allows for some considerable economies of scale whilst retaining some localization. In both cases there have been economic treats reducing to zero tariffs between nations in the region. The North American Free Trade Agreement and the European Union respectively.

- A firm can produce a country version of a product. For example Mister Donut in Japan offers a smaller coffee cup to fit the hand of the average Japanese. Mattel Toys, based in the US, had an interesting experience with their Barbie doll.

  The toy-titan was mystified when despite successfully selling its famous Barbie doll in dozens of countries without any modifications, sales refused to pick up in the Japanese market. Takara, its Japanese licensee, decided to survey eighth-grade girls to account for the resistance from the market.

  The Barbie bloomer soon became clear; Japanese girls could not relate to the doll as her breasts were too big and her legs too long. They modified the Japanese Barbie, and sales shot up. Hardly surprising then, that today, Mattel has made the quintessential blonde bombshell into a demure, dark-haired, sari-clad bride for the Indian market.

- A firm can produce a city version. For example a beer to meet Tokyo tastes.

3 **Product invention** is about creating something new. Research suggests two types. **Backward invention** is reintroducing earlier product forms that are well suited to a foreign country's needs. The National Cash Register Company sold crank operated cash registers at half the price of a more up-to-date cash register and sold large numbers in Latin America and Africa. There is a growing interest in developing products for the developing nations, not only is it a huge potential market but there is a sense that beyond the economic opportunity it is also an opportunity to help

them advance themselves. The second type is **forward invention**, not unsurprisingly, creating a new product to meet a need in another country. This type of invention is also of particular value in the developing world. There is a considerable need in the developing world for low-cost, high protein foods. A number of firms, including Monsanto, Swift Foods, and Quaker Oats are creating new food products to meet this need. What's more, the product, promotion and distribution approaches are typically different. Product invention can be costly but the pay-off can be substantial particularly if the innovation can be used in multiple markets around the world.

COMMUNICATIONS

Firms can use the same marketing communications as in their home country or they can change it for other national markets, a process called **communication adaptation**. If it adapts both the product and the communications, the firm is doing **dual adaptation** (see Figure 9.2).

The starting point is the message that you are trying to communicate. The firm can use one message globally, varying only the language, name and colours. Exxon has used "Put a tiger in your tank" with just small variations everywhere; this is an idea that seems to resonate in every culture. Colours may need to be changed because of cultural taboos. Purple for example, is the colour for death in parts of South America. Whereas it is white in India and East Asian countries and black in the West. The second possibility is to use the same theme around the world but adapt the copy to each local market. Recently there was a Camay soap commercial showing an attractive women bathing. In Venezuela, a man was seen in the bathroom with a wedding ring prominently displayed on his hand; in Italy and France, only a man's hand was seen; and in Japan, the man waited outside. The positioning is the same but the execution reflects local values. The third approach is to develop a global pool of ads, from which each country chooses which would work best for it. Coke and Goodyear have used this approach. Finally, some firms allow their country-marketing managers to create country-specific ads, within global guidelines. Kraft used different ads for Cheez Whiz in different countries. An incredible 95% of Puerto Rico's homes eat Cheez Whiz, and 65% of Canadian households, while in the US it is considered, and we think they have got it right, junk food. If you look at the ingredients of Cheez Whiz, cheese is not prominently featured.

Which media is used and how also may require some international adaptation because media availability and effectiveness differs from country to country. Norway, Belgium, France, Canada and the US do not allow cigarettes and alcohol (except beer in the US and Canada) to be advertised on television. Most developed countries have some restriction on ads for children. Saudi Arabia does not want advertisers to use women in ads, makes you wonder how they advertise bras. Sales promotion is another key communications tool which varies to use and effectiveness. Several European countries have laws preventing or limiting sales promotion tools such as discounts, rebates, coupons, games of chance and premiums.

Another thing to consider is taste. In some parts of the world, misogynist-type messages are still permissible, in others they are not. Groupe Bull, a French IT company, used to own a subsidiary in the US that sold high-speed printers. The CEO, who was not American, recently returned from a visit in Europe with a promotion video to be shown to all their prospective clients in America and as a promotional tool at trade shows. The video featured an attractive woman wearing equally attractive clothing stepping into a sports car, and while driving at fast speeds would change gears in a suggestive manner. Mixing printers and sexual imagery crossed the line of what America considers good taste.

Finally personal selling approaches may have to change as well. The typical North American no-nonsense, let's get down to business approach may not go down well in much of Europe and Asia where building a relationship is critical. Think of Japan, where a no is rarely heard but often subtlety suggested, a "bull in a China shop" approach is not well received.

PRICE

It would be very elegant and simple to have one price for the world, however, for good reason, that rarely ever occurs. Firms marketing internationally, especially, bigger multinationals face several critical issues when dealing with price, price escalation, transfer pricing, **dumping** charges and grey markets.

When firms sell abroad they face **price escalation**. A Dior scarf may sell for $200 in France but $300 in Tokyo. Is this the customer being ripped off? Most likely not. Dior has to add the cost of transportation, tariffs, importer margins, wholesaler margins and retailer margins to the factory price. Plus it is simply expensive to do business in Tokyo where rents are high and so are wages. Depending on these added costs and currency fluctuations the product may sell for two to three times or more what it costs in the country of manufacturer in order to end up with the same level of profit for the manufacturer. In some cases some products in supermarkets are cheaper in the inner city than in a wealthy suburb because they will simply not sell at the higher price point. The price charged by your key competitors provides a very real test to see if you can charge more.

Another issue is **transfer pricing**, that is the price that a company charges to its' own subsidiaries in foreign countries. If it charges too high a price it may end up paying higher tariff duties although it may than pay lower income taxes in the foreign country. If the company charges too little it can be charged with dumping. Dumping is when a company charges either less than it costs or less than it charges in its home market, in order to buy their way into a market or capture high market share. When a country's customs authority finds evidence of dumping it can typically levy a dumping tariff against the firm.

Many multinationals have to wrestle with the problem of **grey markets**, no, this is not marketing to older people. It is where branded products are diverted from normal or authorized distributions channels in one country and sold in another. This happens when there is a substantial price difference between the two countries. In North America quite a large business has sprung up with Americans, particularly elder ones who have a number of prescriptions, coming by bus to Canada to buy their drugs at very large discounts. One seniors website told the story of one couple from Washington State, "After investigating several Canadian pharmacies, my wife and I paid $624.77 for a three-month supply of drugs at Vancouver's DoctorSolve. These same drugs cost us $1,208.04 buying at Walgreen's, Target, and Kmart where we shopped for the lowest prices. That's a saving of $583.27 which includes a Canadian physician's rewriting your doctor's prescriptions – required by Canuck law – personal consultations, and shipping". Grey markets, unlike black markets, are not illegal but are quite irritating to the firms involved because they lose considerable amounts of profit and lose a degree of control of channels of distribution. Multinationals try to prevent grey markets in several ways. Firstly, by policing their distributors, looking for usually high sales, sales figures that don't make sense given their home markets. Another technique is to alter product characteristics or service warranties for different countries. For example you buy a HP printer in Hong Kong at a great price only to find that it's service warranty is only valid in that country. The problem with this approach is that the customer feels ripped off, they bought a perfectly good HP product but can't use the warranty, they should be upset with the store in Hong Kong that sold it to them with mentioning the geographically limited warranty coverage but they will mainly be mad at HP. Many firms try to shut down grey markets. But given the customer unhappiness it creates and the amount of effort required, vendors are learning to accept people do use and pay for their products.

DISTRIBUTION CHANNELS

There is a surprising degree of variation in the ways products get to market in various countries. Selling soap in Japan involves one of the most complex distribution systems in the world. You must sell to a general wholesaler, who sells to a regional wholesaler, who sells to local wholesaler, who finally sells to retailers. With the product passing through all these channel members, the price paid by consumer's ends up doubling or tripling what the importer originally paid. Beyond the length of the channels, the retail end of the system can be quite different as well. Large-scale retailers like Wal-Mart and Sears dominate in the US but in many other countries the retailing sector is more run by small, independent retailers. In India, millions of little shops or just a spot in an open air market are key to moving products. Prices appear high but haggling is the order of the day. Indian incomes are low and many must shop daily for small amounts, cigarettes are often bought singly.

When a firm first enters a country it generally first works with local distributors but as it learns the system it may increasingly venture out on its' own. Over time the firm learns to choose the right distributors for it, invest in them and set-up mutually agreeable performance targets. Some few giant somewhat global retailers are arising, France's Carrefour, Germany's Metro and the UK's Tesco but the vast majority of the world's retailing is still run locally or regionally

SUMMARY

- International expansion starts modestly and continues to grow in size and scale in line with growth.
- Exporters can choose from a variety of such options as joint ventures or licensing agreements to expand internationally.
- Exporters must adapt the marketing mix to suit local tastes and needs of foreign markets.

CRITICAL QUESTIONS

1   Compare and contrast the benefits of using (a) domestic-based export agents (b) licensing agreements, (c) cooperative organizations, (d) joint ventures, (e) the Internet, (f) foreign direct investment

2   It is a basic rule of marketing that the product must be tailored to satisfy customers. Given the diversity of cultures and regional variation within them, why is it that some products like Big Macs for example are the same everywhere in the world? Is the Big Mac the exception to the rule, or a sign of things to come?

3   We have talked about how marketers are mucking about with new tools such as buzz marketing. How can a buzz marketing strategy work in a global market? Should local or global taste-setters be used? Or both? Why?

SUGGESTIONS FOR FURTHER READING

Geert Hofstede, *Cultures and Organizations: Software for the Mind*, New York, McGraw Hill, 2004.

A seminal book in the topic of difference between cultures. A classic which was recently updated. A must read.

Martin Gannon, *Understanding Global Cultures: Metaphorical Journeys Through 23 Nations*, Thousand Oaks, California, Sage, 2001.

An easy to read, entertaining book that has some quite useful messages for marketers. He uses metaphors to help you understand the cultures of 23 nations around the world. A good airplane book.

Kersi D. Antia, Mark Bergen and Shantanu Dutta, *Competing with Gray Markets*, MIT Sloan Management Review, Cambridge MA, Fall 2004, volume 46, issue 1; pp. 63-69.

An excellent recent article which takes a useful pragmatic approach to this important international marketing issue.

GLOSSARY

Active exporting   A commitment to expand the reach of a company into an overseas market.

Backward invention   Reintroducing an older version of a product that is well suited to the needs of a local market.

Communication adaptation   Adapting the communication strategy of a product to suit local conditions.

Contract manufacturing   An agreement between two parties whereby the holder of the trade secret contracts the other party to produce the good.

Cooperative organizations   A collection of producers who sell their product together in order to avoid competing with each other.

Cultural proximity   A term to describe how similar two groups of people are in cultural values and norms.

Domestic-based export agents   A person who sells a domestically produced product overseas on behalf of the producer for a commission.

Domestic-based export merchant   A company that buys a domestically produced product in order to sell it overseas on behalf of the producer.

Dual Adaptation   A strategy whereby the exporter adapts both their product and communication strategy to suit local tastes.

Dumping   When a company charges either less than it costs or less than it charges in its home market, in order to buy their way into a market or capture high market share.

Foreign direct investment   The money spent by an investor to create a business overseas.

Forward invention   Creating a new version of an existing product to suit the local needs or taste of a market.

Joint venture   An agreement between equals where resources are shared for a common purpose.

Lead market   The best performing market.

Licensing   An agreement by a producer to allow an overseas producer to make the same product with the same name for sale.

Occasional exporting   A relatively passive approach to global marketing whereby the producer sells their products overseas intermittently.

Price escalation   The inflation of price of a product sold in an international market compared to the local market.

Product adaptation   The changing of a product to suit local tastes and needs.

Product invention   The creation of a new product.

Psychic proximity   See cultural proximity.

Straight extension   Taking an existing product-line from one market to one overseas.

Trademark   A legally registered monopoly over the rights to a name.

Transfer pricing   The price a company charges to foreign subsidiaries for a product.

GLOSSARY

Active exporting   A commitment to expand the reach of a company into an overseas market.

Activity based cost accounting   A system of assigning costs directly to the resources used in the production process.

Advertising   The placement of announcements and persuasive messages in time or space purchased in any of the mass media by business firms, non-profit organizations, government agencies, and individuals who seek to inform and/ or persuade members of a particular target market or audience about their products, services, organizations, or ideas.

Agenda   The goal an individual wishes to accomplish.

Approaching   The first meeting with a prospect.

Auction pricing   A pricing method where the customer sets their own price according to his or her perceived value of the product.

Augmented product level   The additional services and benefits offered to a customer built around the core benefit and the expected product level.

Average unit cost   The quotient from dividing the total cost into the level of output.

Backward invention   Reintroducing an older version of a product that is well suited to the needs of a local market.

Behavioural segmentation Dividing a market into groups based on the benefit sought.

Black box A term used to describe the process which a buyer undergoes when making a purchasing decision.

Break-even point The minimum number of units that need to be sold to ensure the firm recovers their operating expenses.

Business cycle The period of time consisting of alternating periods of growth and decline in terms of GDP.

Buyer Decision Process A theory that models the steps a buyer experiences when making a purchasing decision.

Buyer's remorse See post purchase behaviour.

Buying centre A word describing the complex system that emerges from decentralizing the authority to buy an expensive product from one person to many people.

Buzz marketing A promotion technique that relies on influencers to speak highly of a product.

Catalogue marketing A form of direct marketing where the seller sends a marketing offer to an interested buyer.

Category killers Vendors that sell so much and so many different products they eliminate niche players that reside within traditional product boundaries.

Channel power The amount of leverage a channel member wields over their partners to elicit cooperation according to their terms.

Closing The step in the selling process where the salesperson requests the prospect places an order.

Cognitive dissonance The discomfort felt by a person when faced with choices that contradicts the individual's personal values, beliefs or attitudes. This conflict drives the individual to select the option that minimizes the tension.

Cold-calling A euphemism meaning calling on the telephone or visiting in person the prospect unannounced.

Communication adaptation Adapting the communication strategy of a product to suit local conditions.

Consumer behaviour The buying behaviour of consumers.

Contract manufacturing An agreement between two parties whereby the holder of the trade secret contracts the other party to produce the good.

Cognitive dissonance A feeling a person experiences when faced with two or more prospects that have conflicting benefits.

Cooperative organizations A collection of producers who sell their product together in order to avoid competing with each other.

Core benefit level The benefit or solution provided by the product the customer is buying.

Core competency A task, skill or resource that enables a company to have an advantage over their competitors.

Cost of capital The rate of return forgone from another investment with similar degree of risk, and maturity.

Cross-ownership A set of producers, wholesalers, and retailers who own shares in each other's companies acting in concert to maximize the returns for the collective.

Cross-promotion A set of partners who combine capital, production capabilities and other resources towards some common promotion objective beneficial to the collective.

Cultural proximity A term to describe how similar two groups of people are in cultural values and norms.

Culture The set of distinctive spiritual, material, intellectual and emotional features of society or a social group, and that it encompasses, in addition to art and literature, lifestyles, ways of living together, value systems, traditions and beliefs.

Customer pyramid A model that proposes marketers segment their customers into classes, from the most profitable to the least, and only target their resources towards those that do or can purchase more products or services.

Customer sales force A sales force structure where each salesperson specializes in selling to specific customers or industries.

Decision maker The person(s) who has the authority to make a purchasing decision.

Demand A call or need for a particular product the consumer desires to satisfy their needs.

Demographic cohort A group of people born in a particular time.

Demographics segmentation Dividing a target market on the basis of social identifiers, such as age, family size, income, gender, education, occupation, religion, social class etc.

Differentiating A strategy a seller uses to distance their product from another by emphasizing its unique features, benefits or qualities.

Differentiation An activity that emphasizes the differences between products.

Direct marketing A marketing strategy tailored around offering convenience, which in turn, builds stronger, more personal relationships between the buyer and selected customers. No intermediary promotion or distribution channels exist.

Direct-mail marketing A form of direct marketing where the seller sends a marketing offer to a prospective customer through the mail, or through the telephone system in the form of a fax, or voice mail.

Direct-response television marketing A form of direct marketing whereby the seller connects to a prospect through the airwaves, either by broadcasting an infomercial, or by advertising their product on a cable shopping channel.

Distribution A word describing the arrangement of a series of data plotted on a graph.

Domestic-based export agent A person who sells a domestically produced product overseas on behalf of the producer for a commission.

Domestic-based export merchant A company that buys a domestically produced product in order to sell it overseas on behalf of the producer.

Downstream stretch A product strategy whereby the vendor moves into a higher volume but lower profit per unit market.

Dual Adaptation A strategy whereby the exporter adapts both their product and communication strategy to suit local tastes.

Dumping When a company charges either less than it costs or less than it charges in its home market, in order to buy their way into a market or capture high market share.

Evaluation of alternatives The third step in the buyer decision process in which the buyer weighs the advantages against the disadvantages of choosing one product over another to satisfy a need.

Exclusive distribution A placement strategy whereby the manufacturer grants a limited number of vendors the right to sell a product.

Expected product level The combined features and qualities of a product that delivers its core benefit.

Fast follower A nimble competitor who can enter profitable markets quickly.

Fixed costs Expenses incurred by the business that remains constant despite the level of production.

Following-up   The final step in the selling process where the sales-person contacts the prospect after completing sale ensuring the customer is satisfied with the product.

Foreign direct investment   The money spent by an investor to create a business overseas.

Forward invention   Creating a new version of an existing product to suit the local needs or taste of a market.

Frequency   The number of times a person is exposed to an advertisement.

Gatekeepers   The individual(s) who recommends a list of vendors who sell products that could be of use to solve a company's needs.

Gender segmentation   Dividing a market according to gender.

Geographic segmentation   Dividing a market into smaller geographical units.

Geographical pricing   A pricing method whereby the price charged differs in different geographic locations.

Going rate pricing   A pricing method used for commodities where the price charged is the same charged by the competition.

Grey marketing   Products sold through marketing channels not approved by the manufacturer.

Gross domestic product   The national production of a country in a year including exports.

Group pricing   A pricing method whereby a group of buyers agree to share resources to increase their bargaining power with a much larger sized supplier.

Groups   Two or more people interacting together for a common purpose.

Handling   The step in the selling process whereby the salesperson answers the prospect's questions or objections.

Hierarchy of effects model   A six-stage model tracing the steps a customer undergoes before.

Human needs   Instinctual urges that must be satisfied. They include physical, social or individual.

Human wants   The item humans decide to consume to satisfy a need given their culture and personality.

Imitator   A person who adopts the habits of an influencer.

Income segmentation   Dividing a market according to income levels.

Influencer   A person who wields influence over a group.

Information Search The second step in the buyer decision process in which the buyer gathers data in order to make an informed decision on how best to satisfy their need.

Initial brief statement A brief that explains your business interests with another party.

Integrated Marketing Communication (IMC) A promotion strategy whereby all promotional activities are coordinated to ensure the consistency and quality of the transmitted message.

Intensive distribution A placement strategy whereby the manufacturer grants distribution rights to any vendor.

Joint venture An agreement between equals where resources are shared for a common purpose.

Just-in-time delivery A supply chain concept whereby goods arrive at a place only when they are required.

Kiosk marketing Placing mobile stands to disseminate corporate information or to collect contact information about a target market.

Lead market The best performing market.

Learning curve A relationship between experience and improvements in efficiency. The more often a task is performed, the less time is required to complete the task.

Licensing An agreement by a producer to allow an overseas producer to make the same product with the same name for sale/

Life-cycle segmentation Dividing a market into different stages of life.

Lifestyle A manner of living reflected in a person's personal opinions, values and choices.

Line-stretching Lengthening the product-line to customers in up or downstream markets.

Loss leaders Deliberately selling a product below cost to attract customers.

Luxury goods A good where rising prices results in a less than proportional drop in demand.

Market segmentation Dividing a heterogeneous market into smaller groups of similar characteristics.

Market skimming Setting the price of a product at the highest possible level, and over time gradually reducing the price to attract new but less needy customers.

Marketing channels An organized network of agencies and institutions which, in combination, perform all the functions required to link producers with end customers to accomplish the marketing task.

Marketing management   The administering of the process of satisfying consumer needs while ensuring the company makes a profit.

Marketing mix   The types of marketing strategies employed to meet an organization's objectives.

Marketing myopia   When marketers lose sight that satisfying needs is driving the consumer's purchasing decision.

Marketing objective   A stated goal a company wishes to accomplish by selecting a particular price for their product.

Markup pricing   A method of pricing whereby the producers adds a premium to the cost of the product to ensure the profit earned will equal at least the opportunity cost of the investment.

Mass-customization   An offering where the customer can tailor a generic product to their tastes.

Massive Multiplayer Online Games (MMOG)   A computer game that enables hundreds of thousands of users to interact within a simulated world via the Internet.

Media fragmentation   A phenomenon whereby market forces are driving media channels to focus on a smaller and smaller sized audiences.

Mission statement   A summary of the stated goals of the organization.

Need Recognition   The first step in the buyer decision process in which the buyer becomes aware that they have an unsatisfied need.

Normalized   A method of transforming data in order to apply various statistical tests.

Normative   The way things are.

Null hypothesis   A hypothesis assumed to be true until proven otherwise.

Objection handling   Having prepared answers to client questions or concerns.

Occasional exporting   A relatively passive approach to global marketing whereby the producer sells their products overseas intermittently.

Opportunity cost   The forgone return from making one investment over another with similar risk profiles.

Oversegmentation   Dividing a market into groups that are unprofitable to serve.

Perceived performance   The gap between the buyer's expectations and the product's performance in satisfying a need.

Perceived-value pricing   Pricing goods according to how customers perceive the value they receive from consuming a product.

Perfect information   A theoretical environment whereby consumers have access to any source of information needed to make an informed decision.

Personal selling   A promotional tool where the marketer uses salespeople to convince interested buyers to spend.

Personality   The sum of qualities and traits, that are particular to a person.

Podcasts   A free audio broadcast available for downloading onto portable listening devices or computers.

Post purchase behaviour   The fifth step in the buyer decision process in which the buyer evaluates how successful the product they chose to purchase was in satisfying their need.

Pre-approaching   Researching information about the prospect's needs and concerns.

Prescriptive   The way things should be.

Presenting   The step in the selling process in which the salesperson pitches the product to the prospect, highlighting the product's benefits.

Price discrimination   A pricing method whereby a different price is charged according to a customer's willingness to pay.

Price escalation   The inflation of price of a product sold in an international market compared to the local market.

Product   A bundle of physical, psychological and experiential benefits that the customer receives that satisfies one or many wants or needs.

Product adaptation   The changing of a product to suit local tastes and needs.

Product-filling   A product strategy whereby the vendor offers the same product in different shapes, sizes, qualities or prices.

Product invention   The creation of a new product.

Product ladders   A mental ranking system a consumer employs to sort products in a particular category.

Product life-cycle   The revenue of a product over its lifetime.

Product mix   The portfolio of products offered by a vendor.

Product positioning   Deliberately crafting a marketing mix separating the product from competitors.

Product sales force A sales force structure where each sales person specializes in selling a portion of the product line.

Product-line consistency The similarity between different product lines.

Product-line depth The number of different packaging sizes of a product.

Product-line length The number of products sold in a product category.

Product-line width The number of different product categories a vendor offers a product to.

Promotion mix The blend of the five tools used by marketers to promote a product.

Prospecting Devising a list of qualified customers who would be receptive to a marketing offer.

Psychic proximity See cultural proximity.

Psychographic Segmentation Dividing a market into different groups based on attitudes, personal values, lifestyles or personalities.

Psychological pricing A pricing method that lessens the cognitive dissonance of making a purchasing decision.

Public relations A promotional tool where the marketer attempts to influence public opinion by releasing one-sided information through news media channels.

Pull strategy A promotional strategy whereby the promotional mix is tailored to attract the target market, who in turn requests distribution channels to supply the product.

Purchase decision The fourth step in the buyer decision process in which the buyer selects a vendor to satisfy a need.

Push strategy A promotional strategy whereby the promotional mix is tailored to push a product through various channels to the target market.

Reach Measure of the effectiveness of an advertising campaign in percentages.

Reference price The price consumers believe a product should be sold at.

Role A set of activities a person is expected to perform in a particular social setting.

Sales force management The analysis, planning, implementation, and control of all activities related to the sales-force. These activities include crafting the structure of the sales department, delegating the tasks conducted by the salesperson, designing the selling strategies employed by the sales force and all actions related to recruiting, training, compensation and evaluation of the sales-force.

Sales promotions   Monetary incentives to make a purchase immediately.

Sales-task clarity   A set of clearly defined responsibilities and expectations for a salesperson.

Segment   A group of customers that share one or many attributes with one another.

Selective distribution   A placement strategy that grants more than one vendor the right to distribute a product, but not every vendor.

Self-cannibalization   A consequence of a Product-filling strategy where the new product introduced eats into the sales or profits of other products offered by the same vendor.

Straight extension   Taking an existing product-line from one market to one overseas.

Strategic Business Unit (SBU)   A semi-autonomous unit of a large sized company, often in charge of setting its own corporate strategy.

Strategic plan   The roadmap that outlines how the goals and objectives will be achieved.

Strategic planning   A process of developing and maintaining a plan of action that coordinates the activities of every business unit to ensure the long-term goals of an organization are fulfilled.

Sunk cost   An irrecoverable expense.

Supply chain   A linear process that maps the transformations of a raw material into a finished good.

Sustained competitive advantage   An enduring core competency that provides lucrative returns for a company over time.

Target market   The market the producer decides to market their product to.

Target return pricing   A method of pricing that ensures the total profit will equal the expected return on investment.

Telephone marketing   A form of direct marketing where the seller uses the telephone to contact customers.

Territorial sales force   A sales force structure where each sales person is assigned an exclusive geographical territory to sell the company's entire product line.

Timing   Releasing an advertisement at a time that minimizes the risk of confusing the audience.

Total cost   The sum of all variable and fixed costs.

Trademark   A legally registered monopoly over the rights to a name.

Transfer pricing   The price a company charges to foreign subsidiaries for a product.

T-Test   A test applied to a null hypothesis claiming a sample size of less than 30 is a t-distribution.

Two-way stretch   A product strategy whereby the vendor simultaneously moves into a higher margin, low volume market and a higher volume, low margin market.

Unique Selling Proposition   A theory which assumes buyers cannot distinguish between products that differentiate themselves along multiple dimensions, as such, it prescribes vendors should differentiate themselves from their competitors by solely emphasizing one feature, quality or benefit.

Upstream stretch   A product strategy whereby the vendor moves into a higher margin but lower volume market.

Utility   The level of satisfaction a consumer receives from making a choice.

Value Added Resellers (VAR)   A company that modifies an existing product in order to add more value to the consumer and resells it to a customer as a new product or service.

Value network   A system of interdependent organizations needed to source, support, and deliver a product that provides customers with the highest level of value.

Value proposition   The offer a producer makes to a customer.

Variable costs   Expenses incurred by the business that change in proportion to the amount of product produced.

Veblen goods   A good where rising prices results in higher demand.

Word association   A type of analysis where the tester prompts the subject for an immediate answer to uncover what types of associations the subject has made with a product.

Word of mouth   When a customer shares their experience of a product with another.

Workload approach   A model that evaluates the total amount of resources used to perform a task.

Z-Test   A test applied a null hypothesis claiming a sample size of more than 30 is a z-distribution.

INDEX

220 INDEX

Management: The Basics
Morgen Witzel

'A valuable addition to the management lexicon - I would urge students of management to read this book.'
James Pickford, *Editor of FT Mastering, Financial Times*

'Witzel has an engaging style which makes this an excellent text for students on introductory business and management courses.'
Kerry Carson, *University of Louisiana, USA*

Management: The Basics provides an easy, jargon-free introduction to the fundamental principles and practices of modern management. Using examples ranging from people management at Cadbury and the Enron crisis to the marketing of fried chicken in China, it explains key aspects of:

- planning effective business strategy to meet goals
- how successful marketing works
- how organizations are structured and function
- how to understand corporate finance
- what affects how people work and effective human resources management
- the importance of knowledge and culture.

This informative and accessible guide is ideal for anyone who wants to understand what management is and how it works.

Morgen Witzel is Honorary Senior Fellow at the School of Business and Economics, University of Exeter, and editor-in-chief of *Corporate Finance Review*.

0-415-32018-6

Available at all good bookshops
For ordering and further information please visit
www.routledge.com